LADYBUGS, TORNADOES, and SWIRLING GALAXIES

English Language Learners
Discover Their World Through Inquiry

BRAD BUHROW & ANNE UPCZAK GARCIA

Columbine Elementary School, Boulder, Colorado
Foreword by Anne Goudvis

Stenhouse Publishers
Portland, Maine

Stenhouse Publishers
www.stenhouse.com

Library of Congress Cataloging-in-Publication Data
Buhrow, Brad, 1962–
    Ladybugs, tornadoes, and swirling galaxies : English language learners discover their world through inquiry / Brad Buhrow and Anne Upczak Garcia ; foreword by Anne Goudvis.
        p. cm.
        Includes bibliographical references.
        ISBN 1-57110-400-3
        1. English language—Study and teaching (Elementary)—Foreign speakers. I. Upczak Garcia, Anne, 1972– II. Title.
PE1128.A2B76 2006
72.652'1044—dc23   2006043314

Cover and interior design by Martha Drury
Cover photograph by Cary Jobe
Interior photos by Cary Jobe, Pamela Towne, and the authors

Manufactured in the United States of America on acid-free paper
11 10 09 08 07 06 9 8 7 6 5 4 3 2 1

This book is dedicated to our students. Not only is it about them, but they are the ones who created it with us. Thank you to all the Columbine Elementary School students who have touched our lives and teaching, making us critical learners of our craft.

CONTENTS

FOREWORD

Daniel and Kent hang up their giant mural of "Snacks for Snakes" on the board as kids gather on the rug. Daniel begins, "We researched all the food and prey that snakes eat. But first I want you to tell me what you know about snacks for snakes."

I'm amazed at this original approach to engaging the audience, but the kids don't miss a beat.

José Carlos pipes up, "I know snakes don't have teeth, except for venom."

"I saw a snake that was longer than a bicycle!" offers Michael.

"Look!" exclaims Tristian. "That boa constrictor on your poster is as long as a school bus!"

"*Tengo una pregunta,*" wonders Mabel. "*¿Qué tan rápido van las víboras?*" [I have a question. How fast do snakes go?]

"I see on your poster a snake that's going to eat a rat!" notes Yok.

Kent explains, "Yeah, that snake is eyeing a sewer rat."

Before Kent and Daniel continue their presentation, they give their classmates sticky notes and ask them to jot down their questions and comments. As the kids concentrate on their writing, I realize that the two adults in the room haven't said a word.

Meaningful learning takes place in an environment that encourages thoughtfulness. Brad Buhrow and Anne Upczak Garcia know that all kids, and especially English language learners, will learn and flourish in an environment that focuses on thinking and understanding. This book shows us how they design and craft their classrooms—linked by a shared door and a common philosophy—to honor and guide kids' learning and thinking.

From the kids' conversation about "Snacks for Snakes," it's clear they know how to participate in a community of learners. After spending their first- and second-grade years in Anne's and Brad's classrooms, these children understand that everyone's a teacher and everyone's a learner. For these kids, learning is all about exploring their passions and interests—asking questions, pursuing answers, and sharing that learning with others. And they eagerly spend weeks reading, writing, drawing, painting, and creating their own books, posters, poems, mind maps, and other projects so that they can teach what they've learned to their peers.

When I began working in Brad's and Anne's classrooms as a staff developer several years ago, my first reaction was to wish that my own kids had spent their primary years with them. Who wouldn't want their kids to spend their days researching, writing, drawing, and thinking about the real world—experiencing Australia's Great Barrier Reef, dangerous insects, or the origins of tornadoes and hurricanes? What better way to begin first grade than with teachers who take kids' thoughts, interests, questions, and ideas seriously? As we've worked to blend comprehension instruction and ELL best practices to make science and social studies come alive for primary kids, it's the kids who have inspired us and taught us where to go next.

Like many classrooms nowadays, Brad's and Anne's classrooms are "culturally and linguistically diverse"—words we use to describe classrooms with an interesting mix of kids from different cultures who may speak a variety of languages. Anne's and Brad's classrooms include kids who are just learning English, those who are native English speakers, and some kids who are well on their way to becoming truly bilingual and biliterate in Spanish and English. Designing and differentiating instruction to meet the needs of each and every kid is a tall order. In their book, Brad and Anne address these challenges head-on. In an era of one-size-fits-all programs and practices, their instruction is focused, explicit, and geared to the needs of kids who have grown up in the neighborhood as well as those who have just arrived in the United States.

The book begins at the start of the school year, as Anne and Brad build on the wealth of experiences kids bring to the classroom. They gently nudge kids, some of whom find themselves in a new and bewildering language and culture, to become increasingly confident speakers, writers, and readers. Children who are at first silent and watchful eagerly begin to tell, draw, and write their own stories because their thoughts, experiences, and feelings are valued. They understand that it's okay to take risks and that learning to read and write is hard but rewarding work.

Understanding is key, so Anne and Brad explicitly teach reading and thinking strategies so that kids connect to, wonder about, and soak up all sorts of new information. The more they learn, the more they wonder, and as the year unfolds, kids' self-selected investigations become a central focus of their day. Working big is contagious in these classrooms—creating striking visuals and text on large paper inspires kids to organize their thinking and take it public. Ansel's volcano spews real pebbles as lava explodes from its top, José Carlos's praying mantis pops up to surprise its prey, the "door" to Jordan's pyramid swings open, revealing the mummy inside. The classrooms burst with energy and enthusiasm.

In every chapter of the book, Brad and Anne demonstrate how they closely observe and assess their students' thinking and learning. They share thoughtful assessment practices and continuums to assess kids' research skills and strategies. We readers get a picture of life in real classrooms with teachers who are consummate learners—constantly reflecting on their own teaching to make a difference for kids.

As you enter Brad's and Anne's classrooms, there's a quote that reads "[L]ike children, teachers grow into the intellectual life around them" (Johnston 2004). The intellectual life of teachers and kids flourishes in these classrooms. Thanks to the kids' curiosity, laughter, and enthusiasm, we learn from them how to teach in ways that capture their joyful learning. So think of all the possibilities for exploring more deeply how kids learn and have some fun while you read this. And listen and watch as kids grow in their thinking, understanding, and learning.

—Anne Goudvis

ACKNOWLEDGMENTS

This book has been a long and arduous process, with support coming from many different facets of our lives. First and foremost we would like to thank the kids for their vivacity and creativity. A toast to Lynn Widger, our boss, who gives us the freedom and trust to do this kind of work. A thousand thank-yous to Anne Goudvis for her constant mentoring and support and to Stephanie Harvey for her advice. Thanks to Nancy Commins for always pushing us to think critically about our teaching. Without Cary Jobe, our photographer, the kids' work would not have been given the justice it deserves. We cannot forget those colleagues who have unconditionally supported us, read our manuscripts, and listened to us as we worked through our writing. Without the support and love of our families and friends this book would never have gotten finished. They were kind and understanding when we had to spend hour upon hour in coffee shops writing and talking about the book. Finally, thank you to our editors, Philippa Stratton and Brenda Power, for giving us the chance to write this book and then guiding us through the process.

INTRODUCTION

The summer has come and gone, and we have left our adventurous souls behind in various parts of the world. It is once again time to settle into the routines of work and the challenges of a new school year. We arrive on the first day of meetings with lingering thoughts of Latin America in our minds. We do not yet know each other, but it turns out we have something in common: we are hopeless travelers. It's a start. We are to be part of a new team at Columbine Elementary in Boulder, Colorado, that is forming part of a restructured program with a bilingual component and a strong ELL component. Our school population is predominantly Latino, we have approximately 87 percent English language learners, and around 85 percent of our student population is on free and reduced-price lunch. There are six people on our team, ranging from one with twenty-five years of teaching experience to novices. We are all very different, and the tension is high.

Anne is thinking, "This is a big shift for me. I finally have my own space with great light, a view, and heat that works" as she sits in the middle of a cold tile floor with nothing but a teacher's desk that was accidentally waxed to the floor over the summer. "I don't know how this is going to go." She is worried about stepping into a new model that is unfamiliar. She has been working in a dual immersion model and is nervous about what this year will bring.

Brad is moving and shifting things around his room across the hall and also wondering what the year will shape up to be like. "When am I going to get some time to talk with my colleagues about what we are going to do since we will have kids moving and being grouped and regrouped from our classes in less than a day's time?" There has been little time for the teams to actually talk. "What are my teammates like? How will they set up their rooms? Do they value publishing kids' work? Inquiry? Sharing?" Thoughts buzz through his head as the incessant noise of the floor polisher hums up and down the hallway.

Luckily, a few hours later we were able to sit down and talk. Over time what has emerged has been a strong working relationship and the idea to write this book. In the beginning we didn't know that we were about to embark on an adventure of defining our educational philosophies and honing our praxis (theory and practice informing one another), nor did we know that it would be a process through which we would be challenged to define and rationalize why we do what we do. In the end it has forced us to do all of these things and more.

As a result of the restructuring of our program our team was built and we were given the chance to work together on developing a common praxis that strives for an educational environment for kids that values their cultures and beliefs, their native languages and their new language, and their thinking. Brad works with students who are ELLs and receive literacy instruction in English but do not receive native language literacy instruction. These can be students from Vietnam, Thailand, Russia, or anywhere where Spanish is not the native language. He also works with students who speak Spanish, but have chosen not to be in the bilingual program. Anne works with students who are receiving both native language literacy instruction in Spanish and ESL-based (English as a Second Language) literacy instruction.

The pages of this book will reveal our own thoughts about one way to approach working with English language learners (ELLs), yet we also believe that many of these approaches are simply good practices and can be successfully implemented with all students. It has been fun and exciting to experiment with different approaches to teaching nonfiction, and we hope it will give others ideas. When we focus on assisting the students in their quest to contribute to the class's knowledge base while working through the writing process, the thinking that comes out is incredible. When we teach kids, they create things we could never imagine, such as colossal whale sharks, giant crabs, swirling galaxies, cirrostratus clouds, exploding volcanoes, ladybug-eating mantids, rocking earthquakes, and much, much more. We hope their thinking and learning will help them act and transform their own world to make it a better place.

ELLS AND NONFICTION WRITING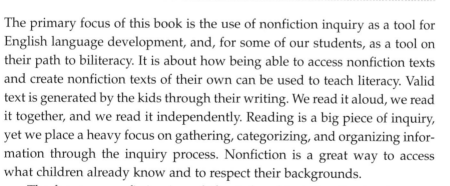

The primary focus of this book is the use of nonfiction inquiry as a tool for English language development, and, for some of our students, as a tool on their path to biliteracy. It is about how being able to access nonfiction texts and create nonfiction texts of their own can be used to teach literacy. Valid text is generated by the kids through their writing. We read it aloud, we read it together, and we read it independently. Reading is a big piece of inquiry, yet we place a heavy focus on gathering, categorizing, and organizing information through the inquiry process. Nonfiction is a great way to access what children already know and to respect their backgrounds.

The focus on nonfiction is multifaceted and includes the development of personal narratives, the leap into inquiry, the gradual-release-of-responsibility model, the teaching of nonfiction conventions, the incorporation of information literacy standards, and the idea that publishing is an ongoing process that includes conferring, editing, revising, sharing, and responding. We use a myriad of second-language-acquisition theories as rationale for our teaching, which drives our instruction. We want to clarify that nonfiction for us includes what the kids know and experience. It is not simply the standard definition of nonfiction texts that one would normally think of. For instance, nonfiction in our world is a letter, a story about the weekend, a poem, and more. It is anything that helps the kids become independent thinkers and lifelong learners and be part of a bigger culture of thinking. Paolo Freire's words sum up what we hope to create in our classrooms.

> *We wanted a literacy program which would be an introduction to the democratization of culture, a program with men and women as its subjects rather than patient recipients, a program which itself would be an act of creation, capable of releasing other creative acts, one in which students would develop the impatience and vivacity which characterize search and invention. (Freire 1970)*

CRITICAL PEDAGOGY AS A GUIDE

Another important facet of our book is that we focus on the idea that the children are the center of our work and approach our teaching through a critical pedagogy model, which traditionally refers to educational theory, and teaching and learning practices that aim to raise the critical consciousness of the student. Joan Wink reminds us that,

> *Critical pedagogy is a process of learning and relearning. It entails sometimes painful reexamination of old practices and established beliefs of educational institutions and behaviors. Critical pedagogy causes one to make inquiries about equality and justice. Sometimes these inequalities are subtle and covert. The process requires courage and patience. Courage promotes change and democracy provides all learners equal access to power. (Wink 2000)*

Critical pedagogy is a way to develop this culture of thinking we are talking about, where students base their learning on critical thinking and questioning. This has been challenging and extremely worthwhile, because it has forced us to reexamine ourselves as teachers and really think about who our children are and where they want to go in their own lives as learners.

DEVELOPING THINKING DISPOSITIONS

We spend significant amounts of time developing thinking dispositions, which are related to habits, desires, skills, motivation, enthusiasm, and interest. Shari Tishman, Eileen Jay, and David Perkins focus on seven dispositions that they recommend cultivating, and we consider these as we work with our kids to instill productive intellectual behavior. They are the disposition to be broad and adventurous, the disposition toward sustained intellectual curiosity, the disposition to clarify and seek understanding, the disposition to plan and be strategic, the disposition to be intellectually careful, the disposition to seek and evaluate reasons, and the disposition to be metacognitive (Tishman, Jay, and Perkins 1993).

THE IMPORTANCE OF THE PHYSICAL ENVIRONMENT

To be able to build such dispositions we also focus quite a bit on the physical environment of the classroom because of the effect it has on thinking and learning. We will share how we set up a low stress environment for ELLs that is engaging. Included in this section are our thoughts and practices about management routines, which set the stage for later work.

CURRICULUM INTEGRATION AND FOCUSING ON ESSENTIAL QUESTIONS

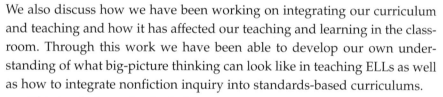

We also discuss how we have been working on integrating our curriculum and teaching and how it has affected our teaching and learning in the classroom. Through this work we have been able to develop our own understanding of what big-picture thinking can look like in teaching ELLs as well as how to integrate nonfiction inquiry into standards-based curriculums.

This is what our day looks like:

Literacy 8:30–10:30
English as a second language/Spanish as a second language 10:30–11:20
Math 12:05–1:05
Content 1:10–1:50
Specials 1:50–2:25
Recess 2:25–2:40
Content 2:40–3:00

The inquiry work happens primarily during literacy, and the content helps launch new inquiries that are at times done during the content hours.

INQUIRY AND INVESTIGATION

The heart of the book takes the readers from start to finish how one might be able to work on a specific inquiry with the kids. We share how to begin by critically reading and questioning nonfiction texts. We then describe how we model the process of reading and note taking and gradually release the students to work independently. We use a specific example of working as a whole group on an inquiry about insects and show how each child then branches off to work on her or his own inquiry about a chosen insect.

KIDS' WORK

The chapter on kids' work is just that—their work. It is packed with samples of what our kids have done over time. The idea behind this chapter is to give people visual examples of what is possible. It is meant to show off the artistic genius of the kids, because they are what keep us going. Their artwork is a valid way for them to make meaning and creates another pathway for them to generate text and make their thinking visible.

LABELS AND DEFINITIONS

We are also very aware of "labels" and spend significant amounts of time discussing semantics with each other and with our colleagues. For this reason we want to clarify that we are using the terms English Language Learners (ELLs) and Culturally and Linguistically Diverse students (CLD) in the text. Although we do not like to label children, we need a way to identify them while writing and think that these two terms embody what we are trying to express.

The American education system has seen a dramatic increase in the number of ELLs in schools since the early 1990s. This increase in many cases has overwhelmed school districts and teachers alike, and the children who are thrust into the system have not always been met with open arms. They are often viewed as inferior to their native English-speaking counterparts because of teachers' lack of understanding about the language-acquisition process. We have overheard conversations that imply that a child is not "up to par," "won't pass the test," or "doesn't have language," or labels such as *struggling, Limited English Proficient, high, low*. We believe these kinds of comments lead to a subconscious inability to instruct and misdirected attempts to fill their heads with knowledge.

Many of our kids are at varying levels of becoming bilingual and biliterate, and as we learn more about their dual language-acquisition process, we are working with them to incorporate their identities into their literacy experiences. For this reason we would like to clarify our definitions of *bilingual* and *biliterate*. A person who is bilingual can speak in two languages with equal or nearly equal fluency, whereas a biliterate person is able to not only speak, but also read and write in both of the languages. Being biliterate implies that the reader has text comprehension and the knowledge of which reading strategies and skills to use in each language, and under what conditions in the languages in question (Singhal 1998).

Politically, immersion in a mainstream English classroom has become popular because of the claim that ELLs who are immersed in English learn it faster. Our program has chosen to do things differently, and we base our work on researchers such as Kathy Escamilla, who have found that ELLs who do not receive support in their native language, or through structured English language development, do not have as much success in the American educational system as some would lead us to believe.

> *. . . transitioned students are expected to have undergone a total linguistic and cultural metamorphosis prior to their arrival in English only mainstream classrooms. Such transformations are not only unlikely, they are not in the best interest of the culturally and linguistically diverse student, and certainly cannot be achieved in three years or less! Thus we see that, far from being a promised land, all English classrooms are often places where CLD students begin to fail, become angry and alienated, and quit trying. (Escamilla 2000)*

We believe it is important to allow the kids to develop bilingual identities if possible. Native language instruction is when students receive instruction in their heritage language. Although we can't provide it for every language group, we are able to provide it for our Spanish-speaking population. Because we work closely with each other, we have begun to see the benefits through the children's ability to transfer knowledge from their native language into English. All of our students will be expected to study in English and do as well as their native English–speaking counterparts at some point during their educational careers. By providing native language instruction as an additive bilingual experience—one where having two languages of instruction enhances the academic experience and strengthens their bilingual abilities—we are making their education a richer experience than it would be if they were simply thrown into an all-English setting with no modifications (immersion). Alienating and frustrating a child is probably the furthest thing from any teacher's mind, but it can happen with ELLs without us realizing it.

We also know that what they learn in their native language can be transferred into another language (O'Malley and Chamot 1990). We see this happening on a daily basis with our students, and it reinforces our belief that the combination of a native language literacy program and a strong English language development program has helped our students.

ASSESSMENT

We use assessment as a tool to guide our instruction. Assessment helps us find the zone of proximal development of each child to help us move them to the next stage of learning, whatever that may be. In the section on assessment we share how we evaluate to plan for instruction. This includes anecdotal notes, transcriptions, inquiry checklists, and so on.

REFLECTIONS

Throughout the book we have inserted our own personal reflections as a way to share some of the harsh realities we face. As we work hard to fine-tune our teaching we often find discord in the profession, and we want to share some of our thoughts with new teachers as well as teachers who may just be beginning their own work with ELLs. In a sense these sections are like "lessons learned."

APPENDIX

The back of the book includes several resources for teachers such as an online resource list and a research guide for parent night (in English and Spanish). We've also included some forms that might be useful, also in both languages.

This has been a great learning experience for us as teachers and learners, and we hope that some of the information in this book will inspire others to delve into a nonfiction literacy pathway.

CHAPTER ONE

CREATING A CLASSROOM ENVIRONMENT

Research with CLD students demonstrates the importance of teachers making a shift from the traditional classroom model where desks are in straight rows and the teacher is in front, to a model of classroom organization emphasizing student centers, and a mixture of guided, group and independent work.—Kathy Escamilla (Miramontes, Nadeau, and Commins 1998)

Omar, Rodolfo, Juan Manuel, and Gerardo are sprawled on the floor, lying in a circle with a dinosaur encyclopedia open in the middle. Brayan is working on his artwork that goes with his research on orcas. His arm moves back and forth as the brushstrokes fill in the glossy black body. Stephanie and Alejandra O. are sitting in the big brown armchair together, reading a fashion magazine, looking for pictures of models to add to Stephanie's information about Milano, Italy, and her research on that country. Daniel is diligently drawing the snacks he has discovered that different snakes eat on his inquiry titled, what else? "Snacks for Snakes." (See color insert 1.) Other kids are outside in the shade reading independently, some are writing in their notebooks, and all of them are doing something based on what they know or want to know. We are conferring with kids individually.

Alejandra Z., who for a long time doodled on her paper, not yet writing the symbols we use to represent words, sits with us and reads. Her English as a second language oral output is emerging, and the school and culture are new to her. She is from rural Mexico and has not been in school before except for a couple of months of kindergarten last year. Her parents registered her for first grade and now she sits silently on the floor with her notebook, looking around at this foreign place. We sit with her to try to tap into her thoughts. Who is she? Where is she from? What does she like to do? After a number of drawings and questions we see that her mother sells tamales, so we encourage her to do a drawing, which she begins eagerly. We bring her a book called *Tamales* in which a young girl is helping her mother make tamales for Christmas. She grabs it with a huge grin and points to the mother. "*¡Esta es mi mamá!*" she says. We browse the book together and she eagerly copies the pictures and writes down some of the words. For Alejandra this moment is pivotal because she has found something that is hers, something she knows about, and something she can share with her classmates that will help them understand who she is. She sees that her world is relevant and important. It is the first step in her wanting to write more.

All of these different things, occurring simultaneously, pretty well describe what a typical day in our classrooms looks like. This kind of cohesion and fluidity has taken a lot of work for us to reach. Every year we are bombarded with testing requirements, kids coming back from vacation thinking about cool swimming pools and melting popsicles—the normal stresses of beginning a year—yet we have been able to keep the big picture in mind, which is the development of a culture of thinking for us and for the kids.

WHAT KIND OF PHYSICAL ENVIRONMENT ALLOWS THE KIDS TO DO THIS?

Our goal when working with ELLs is to create an environment that allows them to take risks without stress. The Affective Filter Hypothesis is one of linguist Stephen Krashen's five hypotheses about language acquisition. He notes that a person learning a new language has a mechanism that either helps or hinders the acquisition process; he calls it the affective filter. The filter can be lowered to allow an individual to be able to access language with greater ease when that person is allowed to study interesting and comprehensible topics; when a student is so engaged in what he or she is doing he or she forgets about the stresses of language (such as forming a grammatically standard sentence); and when the teacher does not push for output production before the time is right. When a child's affective filter goes up, it's because the learning environment has become stressful. The child feels unsuccessful. This can happen if a student is forced to talk when he or she isn't ready to talk; when content becomes incomprehensible or uninteresting; and when the focus of the lessons with the child is on correcting his or her errors.

Creating a stress-free learning environment is not always easy with the resources we have. The lights and computer monitors begin to flicker as soon as Brad's index finger pushes on the mouse to print. In what feels like a possible Category 3 hurricane approaching the school, the power goes out and we're left in the dark. All the lamps, computers, radios, and printers fizzle out, so one of us runs to the breaker box down the hall and flips number twenty-one. It happens often enough that Mickey, our custodian, leaves the door to the fuse box open for us and the kids just keep reading and writing and don't say anything. It hasn't, however, stopped us from dreaming and setting up an environment in our classrooms that oozes *artiste*. We are reinventing our first-grade classrooms and changing them from 1950s cinder-block boxes into reading, writing, and art studios.

When stepping inside a classroom that is a labyrinth of shelves and tables where kids sit on cushions or in armchairs, people sometimes don't understand how we can teach. We know because we used to be them; we had to rethink what we had been taught. We want our classroom spaces to reflect more of a cozy, laid-back environment than a classroom that lacks the natural ambience creativity fosters—an environment that is democratic and promotes thinking.

HOW TO BUILD IT

Low Shelves and Rugs

At the beginning of the school year we think about where we can put shelves to create little breakout areas and quiet places for the kids to read and write. Imagine a room with several nooks and crannies where the children can hunker down with their journals or notebooks, relax, and have a space of their own to think. It is the perfect way to get them to focus and become

FIGURE 1.1
Deysi sits at a low table writing about her pumpkin research.

FIGURE 1.2
Mario works on his mind map about his space research.

independent, free thinkers. To reconvene it is helpful to have one larger meeting area in the room where the whole class can be together. This can be anywhere in the room, depending on the shape and size of the classroom as well as personal preference. We have found that having low shelves helps keep our organized book boxes within easy reach. They also help to keep kids in sight. We like to use rugs of different sizes, shapes, and colors in these areas. It helps to demarcate the space. This year, for instance, one of our kids decided to name the meeting area the red rug meeting area. Everyone knows where that is!

This initial setup looks and feels very different from a traditional classroom that has rows or pods of desks. In a sense it is like using feng shui, the art of designing space that maximizes the flow of energy so that it doesn't become trapped or stagnant, to create a low-stress, comfortable environment where learning and thinking is not only conducive but comes naturally to the children. We arrange and rearrange small spaces if they feel stagnant or the kids don't use them.

Low Tables

Our goal is to create a space for our ELLs that is inviting and comfortable. One way we do this is by providing a variety of different kinds of places to sit and work. We favor tables with the legs removed. (See Figures 1.1 and 1.2.) Often people ask, "Where are the desks?" or "The kids don't have assigned seats?" and even, "But where do they sit?" We place the tables in strategic places around the room so the kids can choose where they want to work. They also have easy access to clipboards, or as Stephanie Harvey and Anne Goudvis say, "portable little desks," if they want to write in a more comfortable place such as in an armchair or on the floor. There are some desks and tables with chairs so the kids can have a choice of where to sit. Setting the room up like this also creates a greater sense of community, because instead of the natural tendency to hoard supplies in a desk, the kids share and have access to everything. This fosters mutual respect for one another and an environment that encourages collaboration, talk, and a nonthreatening, noncompetitive classroom for children who are already under a lot of stress because they are in a new culture, learning a new language.

Kids are no different from adults in that they are able to think better in an environment they find comfortable. Most adults don't like to throw their things down on the floor and have at it, but many kids do. Some kids may want to curl up on a couch with a notebook or paper and clipboard in hand and write away. (See Figure 1.3.) Others do better if they're able to write under the light of the sun—that's right, outside! We are very lucky in that our classrooms have access to outdoor space, so we make that part of our room, creating an outdoor workspace. All it takes is a couple of chairs, maybe a table, or even just a bench. Many of the great writers of our world have been inspired by the outdoors. We wonder how many of them were inspired by a yellow plastic school chair, or being fastened to a desk like we were in elementary school.

FIGURE 1.3
Victor and Jorge settle into a comfy chair in the room to read together.

On Your Own Two Feet

Another option the kids have is to stand while writing. We have several large easels with big chart paper, which are wonderful for young writers. Not only is it different to stand and write, but feeling uninhibited in their motor skills by being able to write in big or small print is liberating. Painters use easels while they paint so they can visualize their work and reflect while going through the process, so why can't writers? When kids are able to stand in front of their writing and work, they tend to talk to one another and share their thinking. It turns into a collaborative process, much like what experienced writers strive for. Having the easels also helps, because the kids can leave their work up and visible while they continue to create.

Mabel had been writing about her family and left her work hanging on the easel. One afternoon her friend Alma approached and asked her what she was doing. The oldest of four siblings launched into a monologue about the members of her family, where they live, how she missed her father because he was still in Mexico, and how her mother was about to have a new baby. The dialog bounced back and forth because Alma also has several siblings, and they began discussing what they like to do with their sisters. This conversation may not ever have happened had it not been for the fact that Mabel's work was visible and she was able to share what she was doing while the information was still fresh in her mind. In fact, we label the work

FIGURE 1.4
Melissa writes her story about playing soccer with her family while standing at an easel.

with placards that say things such as "Works in progress," or "Thinking in progress," or even "Thinking is happening here," which allows other children, teachers, and parents to watch the entire thought process from start to finish. We also hang paper on the walls or whiteboards or on the backs of doors. The challenge is to keep all their thinking organized and presentable.

Highly Visible

We love to keep everyone's thinking out and visible. We used to hide the kids' work away in a corner, or we rolled it up for later use. Sometimes we put all their writing in a folder and seldom came back to it. We noticed that when we left the kids' writing and thinking up and out on tables, their energy to write and read grew. When kids are able to see other writers' thinking, writing, editing, and rewriting, they notice and learn from each other through the writing process. This is important if they are to internalize the fact that their writing doesn't just magically get finished. It takes hard work and time, and it is okay to consult with others about their writing. This kind of consultation creates a community of learners who participate in the learning process together. It's all right if the room is sometimes a bit cluttered and messy, with some books out of place, scraps of paper on the floor, scissors left on a table, a few drops of correction fluid on the table, a dollop of navy blue tempura paint on the carpet. The room belongs to the kids, and we want it to reflect their world and what matters to them. Artists need space and freedom to create, and we try to give them just that.

Set Up a Studio-Like Atmosphere That Promotes Thinking

For us to be able to do all of this work, we began looking at our rooms as thinking studios. (See Figure 1.4.) Once we tape up the first inquiry that someone is working on or has completed, we put some lights, like an art studio with soft track lighting highlighting the artist's work as if to say, "Look at me. Read me." And people do! The kids have such incredible styles in their representations of their text that it's hard not to say, "Wow!" As they read and respond to each other's work, kids start to borrow ideas for what they want to read and explore. The exchange of ideas comes naturally to them. We realized some time ago that we just had to give them time to have those conversations.

CONSTRUCTING THEIR WORLD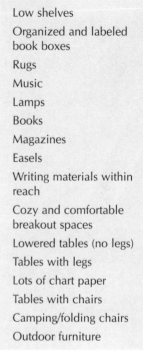

Another question we are often asked at the beginning of the year is "Why don't you have anything on the walls?" This one is easy. We like to use the kids' work throughout the year to fill the walls. We collaborate with them to create visuals that they can relate to, that they have created, and that interest them. Blank walls at the beginning of the year are stark and cold, yet the transformation that occurs is rapid and spectacular.

Tours

We start the year with a tour of the room. "Let's take a tour of your first-grade room. Follow us and we'll talk about your room." We stand up and make our way into some different spaces, thinking out loud. "What should we call this?" Alexia says, "The meeting rug!" We write that on a large sticky note, draw a quick picture, and place the label in an area for all to see. We make our way through all the little areas and name them as we go. Living room, office, and the cozy den are some of the names we come up with. As we take the tour, the kids take turns describing each area and its use. Another thing we like to do so the kids can be confident in giving tours is to practice, so we have them take turns leading the group through the room. Tours happen every once in a while as we discuss the thinking that goes up on the walls. As the tour progresses, we also talk about expectations around the space. For example we ask, "What can you do here?" or "When can we use this stuff?"

We do these tours so that kids know where everything is, can talk about the room, and can generate comprehensible text to define their spaces. (See Figure 1.5.) The kids use their knowledge of their room to give tours to new students, parents, and other visitors.

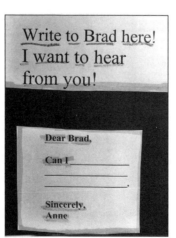

FIGURE 1.5
The message board gives a concrete example of how the kids can structure their notes to us.

To help create an energizing and comfortable space for learning we like the following:

Low shelves

Organized and labeled book boxes

Rugs

Music

Lamps

Books

Magazines

Easels

Writing materials within reach

Cozy and comfortable breakout spaces

Lowered tables (no legs)

Tables with legs

Lots of chart paper

Tables with chairs

Camping/folding chairs

Outdoor furniture

The success of in-school free reading is also consistent with the more general Comprehension Hypothesis, the hypothesis that we acquire language when we understand messages. Recreational reading is, of course, comprehensible input. (Krashen 2004)

Dust Those Books Off!

Each child gets a small plastic book box for his or her personal library. We allow time for them to explore the magazines and books we have in the

FIGURE 1.6
Alden's book box is full of texts he loves to read.

room and the school library. Regardless of reading level, each child chooses texts that interest him or her and that he or she will be able to read during independent reading. The question has come up, "But do all first graders know how to read?" For us, learning to read is simply part of the entire process of learning, so whether they are reading (looking at) images or reading text, we think the exposure to the books is what begins to foster a love for them and a desire to read the words. (See Figure 1.6.) We help them choose books that are "just right" for their level, books they can access independently. We do this by discussing different characteristics of texts that would make them easy, just right, or challenging (Harvey and Goudvis 2000). This is based on a library model where the kids take ownership of choosing books and understand what that involves. Our rooms have Spanish-language libraries and English-language libraries. We have coded the books by placing them in different-colored tubs so that the kids know which books are in English (blue) and which are in Spanish (red). This helps them choose books in both languages and promotes biliteracy in the classroom. This kind of recreational reading is also a way for the kids to have access to comprehensible texts that interest them. Now when we are reading independently, everyone has a variety of books to choose from. We make it a point to help them choose books that are appropriate to their levels and stages of reading, because we have kids who are emergent readers and others who are more advanced. They often start hoarding books, so we limit them to five or six at a time so that they are not overwhelmed, and they are able to carry them. The book boxes allow the kids to read rather than spend their time searching for books. On an individual basis we let the kids search for new books. We find it a fluid system that allows them access to self-selected texts throughout the year and maximizes time we have for reading. The book boxes build a sense of enthusiasm for reading and provide access to books. They really get the kids talking about their reading. It's not uncommon for a group of kids to gather around one book and share it. Rodolfo brought a book from home on dinosaurs in March. The end of May rolled around and all the kids were still trying to find an animal that could beat up a tyrannosaurus rex. Each of the students' tubs has a color picture of the student reading or writing on it for identification not just for the child whose box it is,

but for all of the children. We have even started our own teacher book boxes that we put with the kids' boxes so they can see that we read, too. When all the boxes are lined up, we can see the whole classroom community.

We also have been organizing all of the reading materials from our classroom library in themed boxes, making the contents (books, magazines, comic books, etc.) more accessible to ELLs. We have found that putting the books in small tubs based on a theme, then labeling the tub with a sentence, underlining the important word or words, and including a picture increases a child's access to different kinds of books based on interest and reading development. (See Figure 1.7.) We are also differentiating the texts on the labels to provide for different reading levels. We have been fortunate in that one of our parents has been helping us to draw and write these labels. It takes time, so recruit some help.

If books are tucked neatly away on bookshelves where young ELLs cannot even see the covers, or organized by fiction/nonfiction but not classified, it is harder for them to use the books and magazines, and many of the books might even go unused. Tubs with the books loosely leaning up against one another so the kids can easily browse through them have worked well for us. The kids spend less time searching for books that interest them and more time reading. This also gets them excited about taking books home to read and talk about with their families, which we highly encourage.

Abundant and Accessible Supplies

Pens (felt tip and ink), scissors, markers, paint, glue, staplers, sticky notes, correction fluid, glitter, yarn, construction paper, crayons, chalk, colored

FIGURE 1.8
Labeling the supplies with images helps the kids connect text with the actual objects.

pencils, and felt are some of the supplies we have to work with. We think in terms of abundance rather than scarcity. By this we mean we have supplies available throughout the room, such as five or six jars filled with black, blue, and green felt-tip pens and many containers filled with colorful markers at various places. There is no need to hoard everything in one closet. If supplies are spread around the room, more time can be spent on getting thinking down rather than getting up and going to the one supply area. Each area in the room has a different feel to it when it has accessible materials, and kids can really focus. For example, tables with chairs that have lamps, pens, sticky notes, crayons, and glue might be more project oriented, creating hands-on work, whereas another area with a couch and clipboards within reach may be more conducive to quiet inner thinking and writing. A third area with a table with no legs and comfy chairs might be perfect for kicking back to read. Imagine an artist's studio, with lots of open space and organized mess: paints in jars; brushes dipped in blues, reds, and greens; canvases spread out around the room; and light illuminating paintings. There are sketches of paintings to come on a notepad and unfinished works in the corner. This is the kind of environment we strive for—where creativity and thought explode.

Sticky Notes

We also love to use sticky notes! Initially it may not seem significant in the development of student writing, but there are several reasons why sticky notes are great. First, using small pieces of paper allows ELLs to explore a text, write notes about specific things they see, and stick the notes on the text or image. This helps them remember what they have written about and where that information is. They also help young writers become aware of what they are writing because it has to be concise. Second, it forces them to physically move the notes from the book onto the note-taking sheet into the appropriate column, which helps them synthesize and internalize the information. The use of different colors also helps them organize their thinking. For instance, yellow sticky notes might be used to write questions, blue ones for connections, and pink to document new information learned. Third, it's fun! Kids like to use different kinds of materials when working, and sticky notes come in all shapes, colors, and sizes.

Pens, Pens, Pens

Having the kids use pens is much better than pencils, for several reasons. The most obvious of these is the problem of erasing. When an emergent ELL writer feels insecure, the first instinct is to erase what he or she has written. This destroys not only the paper, but also evidence and a history of their thinking and approximations, which is invaluable for us to see when evaluating that student's writing process. (See Figure 1.9.) We model the use of pens so that the writing doesn't get scribbled out. For instance, when we make a mistake, we model drawing one line through the word or phrase rather than scribbling it out entirely. Additionally, pencils are noisy and distracting. It is probably safe to say that the relentless noise of a child grinding a pencil in a manual sharpener or burning the motor on an electric sharpener can grate on one's nerves and is in fact a distraction to the other kids who are working.

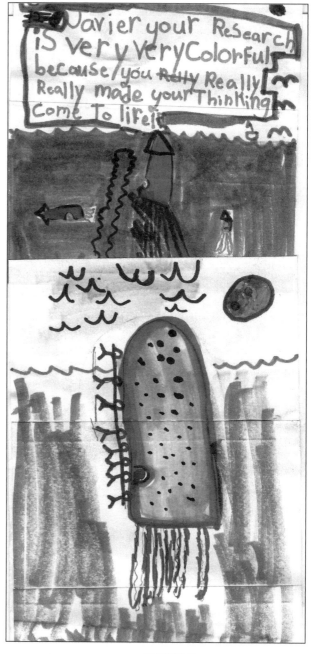

FIGURE 1.9
We note what Cloe is thinking when she crosses out "relly" to rewrite it with a pen.

Labels in Context

Using classroom labels is another simple way of encouraging reading. Everywhere you look there is print that makes sense because it is in context.

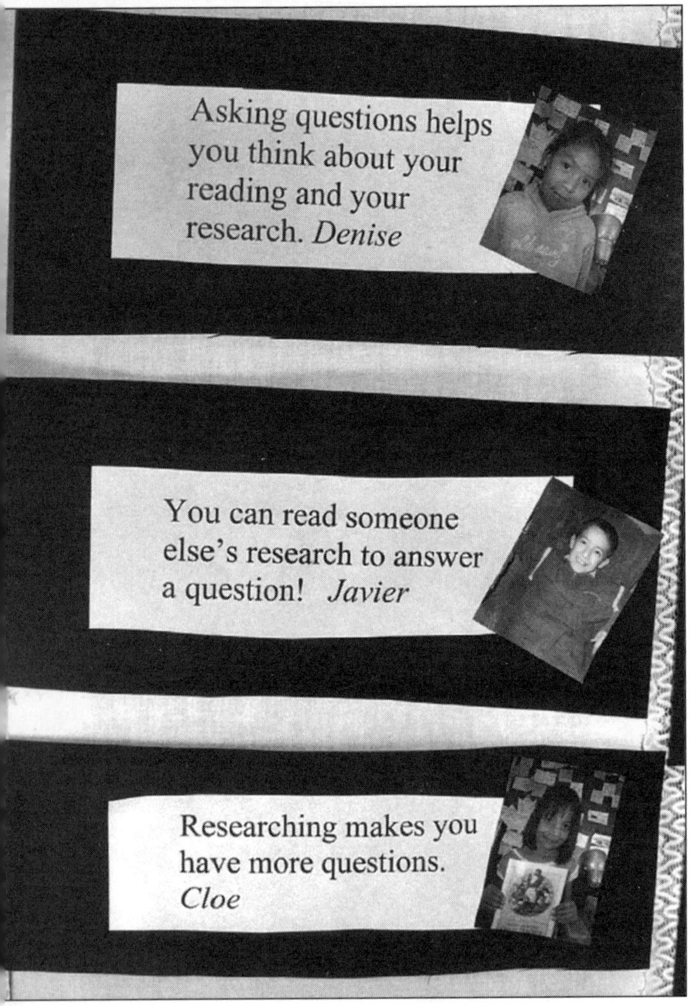

Asking questions helps you think about your reading and your research. *Denise*

You can read someone else's research to answer a question! *Javier*

Researching makes you have more questions. *Cloe*

FIGURE 1.10
We post what kids say to add to the environmental text of the room.

This helps ELLs find what they need because they see both the text and the image. We want to create an atmosphere where thinking and creativity are paramount. We want the kids to feel that they will get what they need when they need it. We put every label in context so kids can see the syntax and vocabulary involved. For a box of nonfiction books we simply write, "Here are some great *nonfiction* books about *wild animals*. Read these to get *information*." Or for markers, "This box has a lot of colorful markers you can use for your *publishing*." Each label is accompanied by a small image. Eventually the kids make labels with visuals for things, often on their own.

"Should we make some little signs to help people new to our room understand where things are?" we say. After our tour of the room we go back and make some signs. We make a quick list of what we came up with, writing "living room" on the paper and making an illustration as an example. We then discuss what we can do in each place. Can we read, write, work on publishing? We take a small square piece of paper like the kids will use, and quickly draw a picture of a person writing in that space. With a few markers we color the image, and with a quick explanation, we glue it to the sign. We take turns illustrating the signs. Cutting out little squares of paper allows all of us to create a small visual to go with each sign.

Environmental Text

Part of the ambience of our rooms is the different kind of texts that the kids are exposed to. We love to type up what they say. The room is filled with kids' quotes on just about anything. (See Figure 1.10.) Flipping through the pages of this book you will see some of the fabulous things they say. We document them so that they see themselves as people who have important things to say. This goes hand in hand with the quotes from researchers, philosophers, educators, politicians, and poets that are posted around the room to remind us of who we are and where we want to go. We also keep our professional development books out for the kids to see that we, too, read and enjoy it. They see the rows of books displayed with the covers forward that we use to inform ourselves about our teaching and know that it is part

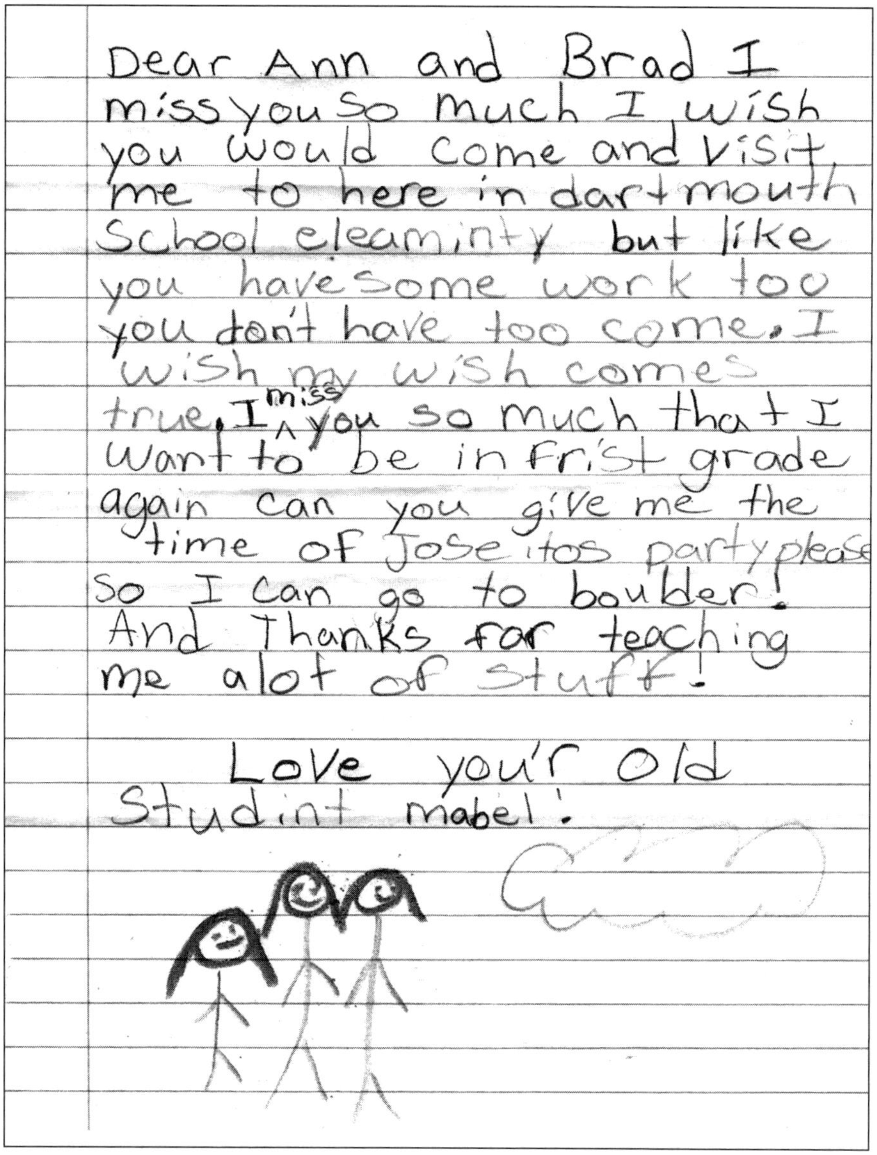

FIGURE 1.11
A letter from a former student.

> Dear Ann and Brad I miss you so much I wish you would come and visit me to here in dartmouth School eleaminty but like you have some work too you don't have too come. I wish my wish comes true. I miss you so much that I want to be in frist grade again can you give me the time of Joseitos partyplease So I can go to boulder! And Thanks for teaching me alot of stuff!
>
> Love you'r old Studint mabel!

of the process of becoming a lifelong learner. The kids will often see our colleagues browsing through our collections and notice how we share and collaborate with each other.

Another way we use rich texts is through the news board, where the kids bring in interesting or exciting stories from newspapers and magazines to post and share with others. Also, the kids display their own books at the front of the room on a low table for the entire world to read and enjoy. Students, teachers, parents, and visitors often come in, and the first things they pick up to read are the books authored by the kids. We also save correspondence from the kids and post it around the room. (See Figure 1.11.) Sometimes former students write to us, current students create elaborate letters with illustrations, or posters about us materialize during free-choice time. It is important to keep this stuff for everyone to see. All of these things contribute to an environment where print is valued and used by everyone.

TAKE A RISK

Organization of our classrooms is important to all of us who use it every day, particularly the kids. The way that we have chosen to set up our rooms may not be for everyone, but it has been extremely successful for us, and we encourage others to try it. To be able to think about changing our rooms we had to unlearn the way we traditionally thought of the physical space. From our own growing up, we were accustomed to classrooms with little on the walls except for bulletin boards created almost entirely by the teacher, desks in neat rows or pods, the floor immaculately clean, and books lined up on the shelves, barely visible to us as children. Once we started to change, we kept in mind that we wanted to create an active place for thinking. Often we hear, from parents, other adult visitors, and even other teachers, that the stuff hanging from the walls and ceiling is in their (the adults') way.

Brad had a friend stop at school one day after the kids had gone home. He said, "Wow," as he was looking around taking it all in. Then he said, kind of talking to himself, "I guess it doesn't really matter if this stuff is hanging that far down. The kids are pretty small so it's not in their way." Brad looked at him and said, "You understand."

A PERSONAL REFLECTION

One afternoon while we were writing this book in Barnes & Noble we had a mini-epiphany. Real live adults actually like to sit in big comfy chairs, sipping lattes while they think. We were relaxed and free to think without feeling tied down to our desks (which we actually don't have in our classroom!), in essence to the system. Barnes & Noble figured this out fast, launching a multibillion-dollar business using the concept of a low-stress community/homelike environment where clients can hang out for hours reading books while snacking, without any obligation to buy. It was nice for us to see a real world example of our own thinking about physical environments and how they can foster reading and writing.

CHAPTER TWO

CREATING A CULTURE OF THINKING

Kent has his poster taped to the whiteboard and is ready to share his information. He has created a giant crab with pieces of paper colored like spikes sticking out to give his creation a multidimensional element. The kids are sitting close to him and are eager to hear his sharing. After he reads and discusses all his words and art, he asks the group, "Do you have any questions, comments, or connections?" Immediately thumbs pop up at the kids' chest level, and Kent can clearly see who would like to respond. Kent makes eye contact with Mabel, who goes on to tell him what she finds interesting about his work.

"I really like your arrows [referring to his notes on king crabs]. Why did you use them?" (See color insert 6.)

"I was putting the pincers and the exoskeletons together. I drew the arrows to show they are both hard. Thank you, Mabel." Kent makes sure he acknowledges her before he moves on to the next person with a thumb up. This is how we interact with each other.

Our goal is to make an academic environment where all inquiries are valued and kids have the dispositions or the attitude and inclination to work independently. When we say this, we mean that the students not only want to use their skills, but also know when to use them. To do this we focus and put energy into developing thinking routines in our classrooms (Ritchhart 2002). With these routines we set the course for self-selected inquiry.

Routines for conversations and learning together at the beginning of the year and practicing them throughout the year help us lay the path for the children to maximize their time for inquiry, second-language development, and exploring information through reading, writing, and conversations. Established routines minimize the time we spend worrying about interruptions, distractions, and discipline issues.

When we refer to thinking routines, we are talking about different ways in which learners can express their thinking orally, in writing, through illustrations, painting, or other art forms. Our goal is to help ELLs build communicative competence. When we explicitly teach these routines in our classrooms, it is much easier for our ELLs to share their ideas and thoughts with us and their peers. Routines facilitate self-expression, because kids focus on what they want to express.

We spend a significant amount of time modeling and practicing thinking routines. Through modeling, our goal is to have the kids acquire both dispositions of thinking and routines and apply these to their own learning. We strive to help them know when to apply their knowledge and abilities.

For example, Vanessa created an inquiry poster on ladybugs, where she began her work in English and continued in Spanish. It was the first time she had decided to work in two languages on the same project. As she worked, we frequently talked about her bilingualism and how she could use it to express her thinking through her work on ladybugs. A couple of weeks later she sat down to write a book. As we conferred with her, she said, "I like to write. I also like to write in English and in Spanish because I'm learning how to write in both." She is aware of her thinking and her competence in two languages. Too often kids think "success" means pleasing the teacher, so they try to copy us. The goal is for the kids to build a repertoire of strategies and make them their own. We want them to become independent, critical thinkers and lifelong learners.

GRADUAL RELEASE

The gradual release of responsibility is our framework for instruction (Pearson and Gallagher 1983). Using this framework we scaffold instruction by using explicit teaching; modeling and demonstration that leads the students through guided practice. When they are ready, we release them to try it on their own (independent practice). Finally, we share and follow up.

> **BENEFITS FOR ELLS**
>
> **Gradual Release Framework**
>
> ✓ Explicit modeling shows ELLs what they are going to be doing in a clear and straightforward manner.
>
> ✓ Practicing allows ELLs to see other students taking risks and lets them interact with peers. Sharing allows for discourse and practice speaking, listening, and reading. In addition the gradual release framework does the following:
>
> > Promotes oral language development as well as reading and writing
> >
> > Creates opportunities for the teacher to scaffold language for many different levels at the same time
> >
> > Builds bridges between group work and independent work in a nonthreatening manner
> >
> > Empowers children with confidence from seeing "how to do it"
> >
> > Allows the teacher to quickly and easily assess a child's understanding in any given lesson and use independent practice time to pull small groups of kids together to differentiate instruction

To better meet the needs of our ELLs we have modified this framework to include activating background knowledge (schema), previewing vocabulary and lesson objectives, extensive modeling and asking kids to notice what we do, guided practice, collaborative/independent practice, sharing, and reviewing vocabulary and lesson objectives.

Activating Background Knowledge, Our Schema

When readers activate their schema, they make connections between what they already know and the new information they are reading to enhance comprehension or to create new learning. Accessing background knowledge and experiences, or schema, helps ELLs make a connection to themselves, their lives, or something they know that gives them greater access to the texts (Miller 2002).

We start working on this from the very beginning of the year through a variety of approaches. We choose texts that we hope kids will have a connection to so they can have discussions about what they know, whether school, their lives, their families, or anything else. By having these discussions the kids start to think about what they know and realize that they know a ton! Having this realization is the first step to accessing their own schema, being conscious that they have a wealth of knowledge and experiences that they can build upon. The next step for them is to use this schema to begin telling, writing, and reading their own stories. By being given the opportunity to share these stories, they are working on discovering and developing their identity within many different contexts.

We Preview

With each lesson we preview what we are going to do by making the objective clear, previewing vocabulary, and discussing what to expect. With more emergent learners of English this kind of preview may be more extensive and include a quick practice of language frames, the use of more detailed images, or even realia. It can be done in five minutes, before the start of the lesson. This way they know what is coming and have recently practiced it, which gives them the opportunity to participate more fully.

Modeling and Thinking Out Loud

Thinking out loud, or making our thinking visible to the kids, is an explicit routine that gets kids into the habit of expressing their thoughts. Through this process we are showing what's important to us, what we wonder about, and what we are interested in and passionate about. Thinking aloud is very effective when writing for the kids, because we demonstrate how we work through our ideas and it helps us gain an understanding of what their process is. We tell the kids that writers have inner conversations like readers do and that we are going to share those inner conversations, so we keep track of our thinking.

Before we model, we prompt the kids to carefully watch us. Afterward we ask them, "What did you see us do?" This is a great way to get them to pay close attention and articulate the thinking strategies we model. We provide a language frame that says, "I noticed you _____" or "I saw you _____." This helps the ELLs quickly access words in English so they can share their thoughts.

The kids are using metacognition to notice thinking. As we gradually release them, we will notice their dispositions, too, such as their eagerness to take an image to start writing or their diligence in sitting down and writing right away. (See Figure 2.1.) Our mini-lesson wrap-up is a simple restatement of the objective and our observations of what we notice the kids doing, such as, "I noticed you talking and thinking, drawing, writing, and making your thinking visible." We do this to turn the tables and notice what they do, which helps make it a reciprocal learning environment.

FIGURE 2.1
We track what the kids notice by talking, thinking, and writing it down.

We like to use pictures to get the kids thinking and wondering about a subject. During our Alaska unit we tape a laminated image of Denali to the easel, our markers in hand. We tell the kids sitting on the floor to pay close attention and notice what we do. We might say, "Watch and listen carefully, because in about four minutes you are going to do what we do." We keep it short, because in the past we modeled for so long, the kids never had time to practice! Now we turn back to the image. First we write some comments on a sticky note and stick it right on the image.

Looking and observing the snow on Denali we might say, "I wonder why there is snow on the mountain in the summer." We go through a number of different examples, always talking about our thinking and then writing it down and accompanying the text with a quick sketch. When asking questions we try to be consistent with our use of language, so we write, "I wonder _____."

"Hmmm, there is so much more we could write, but we want to give you time to explore your image," we say. "Before we do that, think about what you noticed us doing. Take a minute and think." We point to our head. "Now tell someone next to you what you noticed us doing." We scoot through the group and listen in, writing down what we hear and who said it. Quickly we regroup and share. Mariana noticed us looking and wondering. Kent noticed us writing our thinking down. We write these observations down as well. By observing what we do, the students are seeing thinking routines made visible.

Language Frames to Scaffold

We model language frames to scaffold ELLs' written and oral language. We have found that ELLs can be reticent about expressing themselves if they aren't completely confident in what they are going to say or write. By providing them with some structure we help alleviate some of this stress and give them a tool to help them express themselves. Language frames are easy to differentiate and incorporate into our instruction. We usually write them quickly on a sentence strip or on the whiteboard and practice them with our ELLs so that they have access to one way of expressing their thinking.

We use these language frames to help our ELLs gain an understanding of standard English and its structures. When we are developing the language frame for a lesson, we take into consideration that ELLs need to practice things such as simple statements; sentences with nouns, verbs, and gerunds; prepositional phrases; conjunctive phrases (*and, but, because*); comparisons of idioms versus a more formal register; modals; conditionals; contractions; and more (Gentile 2003). The frames can be open-ended so they can be used as a scaffold, and we model what we might use to complete such a frame. For instance a frame to practice conjunctive phrases might be "We are taking notes and _____." We would model how to complete it by thinking aloud and writing, "We are taking notes <u>and</u> making our thinking visible."

Here are some examples of language frames we might use to scaffold English language development:

I see _____. (simple statement)
I like your research because _____. (conjunctive phrase)
Butterflies fly from _____ to _____. (prepositional phrase) Examples
   might be "Butterflies fly from flower to flower," "Butterflies fly

> from Mexico to the United States," "Butterflies fly from cold weather to warm weather."
>
> I am making my thinking visible by _____. (practicing use of nouns, verbs, gerunds or present participles)
>
> I wonder why _____. (transformed statement) or Wow! I learned _____.

We can also practice using this kind of grammar by writing the phrases out and reading them together, then putting pictures with the words. For example, we might create a graphic with a picture frame for the kids to draw in and text typed out below that serves as a caption (see Appendix). The text might say something like "Tornadoes and hurricanes both cause damage." The kids can use this later to build new phrases such as "Tornadoes and hurricanes both have strong winds," or "Tornadoes and hurricanes both cause debris to fly." Language frames can be expanded and practiced orally through a think-pair-share.

We do this type of language scaffolding with content units as well. For instance we might practice adverbial phrases by working on something like "The ladybug landed gently on the leaf." Or an adjectival phrase, "The red ladybug sat on a green leaf." The kids create images to go with the phrases. As they gain more experience, they begin creating their own phrases and art to go with them. With more practice the kids begin to use these language structures in their writing and discourse.

Guided Practice

In guided practice there is a joint responsibility with teacher doing and students helping and students doing and teacher helping (Pearson and Gallagher 1983). This works well for us because it provides a framework for our ELLs in which they have the time and space to both watch and participate.

Think-Pair-Share

As we move into guided practice we ask kids to rehearse their thoughts with a partner before sharing with a larger group. Think-pair-share is a routine that provides ELLs with opportunities to practice talking in a comfortable environment with their peers. We use think-pair-share in large or small groups to encourage more think time and reduce competition. This routine is simple to put into practice. We ask kids to respond to a question or to do their own thinking.

To get the kids to focus on thinking we sometimes point to our head and say, "Now take two minutes and just think. I'll tell you when to share. If you think you're going to talk, put your finger near your lips like this." We make

By inviting students to look for common stories and to debrief them as "texts," we lift the discussion to a higher level of analysis and synthesis and thereby begin to turn individual stories into a larger aggregate meaning.
(Echavarria and Graves 2003)

the "shh" symbol with our finger to our mouth. After the time is up, we say, "Now find someone near you and take a couple of minutes to share your thinking." We move about the group and listen in on all the conversations. Sometimes we write down what we hear and share it with the group; other times we share out loud and write what the kids have to say.

Wait Time or Time to Think

We know wait time is important, but it really didn't hit home until the tables were turned and we were the students. When Brad was studying Spanish in Mexico, he was asked a question in the past tense. The question was in a form that he hadn't heard, so in Spanish, he said he didn't understand. The teacher then asked him again. Just as he was about to get it, a student from across the table jumped in and told him in English what she had said. This did not help him but did frustrate him. The situation really made it clear how important it is to give the kids time to process questions or input. It also gave Brad a great deal of empathy for our students when a teacher or student answers or talks for them when they don't ask for it. When in doubt, wait a little longer, and then help.

Collaborative/Independent Practice

Once we have practiced together and we know that kids understand the task and are clear about what they are to do, it's time for them to try it themselves.

Conferring

As kids practice on their own, our goal is to confer with as many of them as possible. One of the greatest challenges in any classroom is being able to work one-on-one with a child and feel confident that the other children are working on something meaningful. We have had to unlearn the need to control and relearn giving trust, freedom, and responsibility to explore. We have learned that we need to take risks in how we teach. The other part of this is the importance of being able to work individually with ELLs. These students need our attention, and we need to take the time to sit with them so that we can base our instruction on their needs. If we don't know where they are in terms of their thinking and second-language development, we won't be able to meet their needs.

How We Support Kids to Work Independently

We make it clear from the beginning that our students have several choices of what they can do during the time we are working independently. We write them down and post them in the room for all to see so that when they need to refresh their memories, they can simply look at the poster. Giving them the freedom to choose what they want to do has also been liberating because it fosters an environment of thinkers and learners. The kids are all doing different things, but still consulting and sharing with one another and with us. Sometimes we're asked how we keep track of everything that is going on. Actually it is less stressful than trying to control everything all the time because we have to go with the flow. Kids have to learn to take responsibility for making some of their own choices and decisions, because they know not to interrupt us if we are working with another student. We meet each child's needs by working with him or her and guiding him or her to the next level. Once the structures are in place, the kids are more independent. We do not have to orchestrate their every move because they can make decisions about their own learning. They don't depend on us to do their thinking for them.

Time to Think, Wonder, and Discover

Kids need time to read, write, and think, period. Anyone who has written anything knows that it takes time to think and organize your thoughts. Making the time available in our packed days is critical if we expect kids to get their thinking down. It is also an important part of what we do with our kids and part of what we see as the big picture. Without it nothing would ever get done, and when working with ELLs it is an important piece of the writing puzzle.

When thinking about how important time is in reading and writing in life itself, we think of Nobel Prize winner Gabriel Garcia Marquez and his book *One Hundred Years of Solitude*. The story is constructed so that time is seen in a cyclical manner rather than as linear. There is no beginning, no end, simply a symbiotic ongoing process where the writer and his words interact with the world. This is what writing really is, and without the component of time writers cannot be born.

Leslie is an emergent ELL writer. She has relatively strong oral language and listening skills, is an advanced reader and writer in her first language, Spanish, and is extremely confident in her academic abilities. Yet when it is time for her to write in English, she often freezes up. Part of her difficulty comes from being a perfectionist, so to get her to relax, we have had to allow her ample time to write. Her research project on koalas in English has taken much longer to complete than her projects in Spanish. One might think, "Well, of course it does, she doesn't speak English," but that is not the case. We believe, instead, that her thinking process is taking longer and that her confidence is not as great. So we have given her as much time as she needs. She may spend forty-five minutes one day, taking notes from her books, and

---

What do the other kids do while we individually confer with students?

Read books, magazines, and other materials for information.

Take notes on sticky notes.

Plan their writing.

Write their thinking down on paper (in their writer's notebooks, in rough draft format, or publishing).

Publish.

Illustrate.

Make meaning with their art.

Investigate on the Internet.

Confer with other students.

Go to the library to explore topics and look for materials.

That's how writing is too. . . . Through practice you actually do get better. It is odd that we never question a football team practicing long hours for one game, but in writing we rarely give ourselves space for practice. (Natalie Goldberg 1986)

only five the next. She is following the same process she does in Spanish in terms of the steps in the inquiry process, but she is doing it little by little. Once she got rolling, she couldn't stop and in fact wanted to keep writing later that day.

Thumbs

We have been frustrated in the past by kids throwing their hands in the air, competing for attention. At first, hands wildly waving and inching higher and higher until the kids were practically jumping up and down seemed great because at least, we thought, the kids were engaged. But when kids use thumbs and keep their hands low so only the facilitator can see, competition remains low and thinking time increases. (See Figure 2.2.) Ideally we would like to have a natural conversation flowing without any such signal, but for now, so everyone can focus attention on one person at a time, thumbs are a great way to signal, "I have something to say."

FIGURE 2.2
Roberto waits to share his thinking.

One time early on Brad bumped his chest a bit with his thumb, and almost immediately half the room was acting like Tarzan, banging their thumbs against their bodies. Now we're more careful. We look around at the kids gathered on the carpet, most of whom have their thumbs up and are looking at us.

Our goal, too, is to have the kids take over and facilitate in a variety of settings. Using something as simple as thumbs, or choosing someone with eye contact instead of raising a hand, is easily done when the kids share or do a shared reading, and they have fun with it.

Eye Contact

Eye contact is another noncompetitive way to conduct classroom management. It is a quiet way of interacting and calms a group's energy, because it is interactive on a very personal level. Teachers and students have to be focused on one another to be able to communicate with just the eyes. It also gets the kids looking and interacting with each other instead of always depending on us to answer everything, which is very important. For example, when we're in a circle, the kids interact with each other. Our conversations are not just teacher directed; the kids talk with each other.

It's September, and we are gathering together for a modeled write-aloud and mini-lesson on editing. We begin reading aloud as a signal for the kids to come over to the large meeting area. We continue reading until everyone is sitting on the carpet. As we begin our discussion, some kids are playing with the carpet, others are sitting at an angle reading Jordan's Chinese New Year inquiry poster, and a couple of kids are looking at us. We continue, "Hmm, what could we write about?" We go through steps that the kids will face in their writing process. After we've written and self-edited, we turn it over to the kids.

"Let's see, the information makes sense to me. Could someone help me edit my paper?" We make eye contact with Mabel, and Mabel helps us out, saying, "You need to remember to write the date."

For those kids who are not looking at us we simply look and wait until they focus their eyes our way. Sometimes a classmate will help them by calling their name. We address the calling-out help this way: "Remember, we are going to look at you with our eyes, so you really need to be looking and focus your attention here," or "We're going to look at you with our eyes, so if you have something to share, you need to be looking at who is talking." Active listening and what that looks and sounds like in a group is some-thing we are always working on. By active listening we mean that one is participating and thinking about what another person is saying. We used to call kids by their names when we were in a large group, but now we just use our eyes. Using our eyes to choose someone to share forces the kids to really look at the person facilitating the discussion or presentation if they have something to share. It is a routine that we practice consistently in all aspects of management, so the kids get the hang of it quickly.

Anchor Charts

Anchor charts record past learning and guide future teaching (Harvey and Goudvis 2000). We constantly create anchor charts and add to them throughout the year. They evolve over time and are a record of our teaching and the kids' thinking. Even more, anchor charts support the disposition to plan and be strategic (Tishman, Jay, and Perkins 1993). Often, we use quotes from the kids to build the charts. We work together with the kids to make them so that the charts reflect their thinking. Depending on where they are with their writing, we either write their thinking or they write it down and then make illustrations representing their words. Interacting with and creating an anchor chart helps internalize our points of thinking, and when kids create an anchor chart with their own images and words, they own it. (See Figure 2.3.)

FIGURE 2.3
We build questioning anchor charts with the kids and constantly refer to them. Anchor charts support the disposition to be planful and strategic in our thinking.

When building an anchor chart for choosing texts, we:

- create an anchor chart of different ways to choose texts;
- put examples of the kinds of text features that might be easy, just right, or challenging. For example, pictures accompany words, size of text, the amount of text, our schema about the subject, and so on;
- model our own reading choices;
- discuss strategies we use to choose texts, such as whether or not we have schema about the subject, whether it interests us, and whether we understand the text (Harvey and Goudvis 2000).

Conversations Matter for Thinking

"Italy is the beautifulest country in the world," Stephanie tells Alejandra. "It has all the models!" She diligently cuts out pictures of fashion models and glues them next to Milan on the giant map she is making. For each city she has different pictures to represent what she has learned during her process. Venice's streets are made of water, the pope lives in Rome, a volcano destroyed Pompeii a long time ago. She points to the different cities as Alejandra sits with her journal in her lap, watching and listening to her friend. Then she jumps up. "Why not put a moving car in Rome? I've heard there are cars in Rome." She runs over to an inquiry about a praying mantis that José Carlos did several weeks earlier. "See how he made the mantis so it can move?" They stand together in front of the giant poster trying to figure out how he had made his mantis move. Then Alejandra goes to one of the art shelves and pulls some string from a box. "I know. Come." They sit down together and experiment with how to make a moving car. Later, Alejandra sits down to write about her experience with Stephanie.

To the casual observer it might seem like the kids were just talking. Alejandra and Stephanie were constructing meaning and scaffolding each other's learning. We know that when we talk, we bounce ideas off each other, and the kids do, too. If we want to get them excited about what we are studying, then we need to let them get involved in helping us learn it, and they can do this with their inquiry.

Talk and conversations are very important in getting kids to feel comfortable about thinking, reading, and writing. Thinking about conversations and how they occur in our school day is a lot more complex than we once thought. Classroom conversations matter and are key to the development of language and thinking. "Talk, whether internalized self-talk, overt conversation, or writing, is one of our principal mechanisms for organizing our thoughts, making sense of new ideas, and pushing our thinking in new directions" (Ritchhart 2002).

When we begin sharing or talking about a particular topic and start with thumbs, the kids jump in fairly soon and the interaction takes on a more informal format, with the kids having natural conversations. The conversations are reciprocal, and we as teachers participate with the kids rather than it being one-sided (either all teacher or all kids). We aim to be participants and mediators in conversations instead of just facilitating. That is, we share our thoughts and feelings about topics as members of the group, we take risks along with the kids. To the casual observer this kind of conversation (give and take) in school might seem chaotic or unstructured, but for us it is simply a step toward learning how to carry on conversations where individuals take turns listening and speaking and respecting one another's opinions. When the group conversations get animated, we can see

Learning to orally produce an alternate form is not principally a function of cognitive analysis, thereby not ideally learned from protracted rule-based instruction and correction. Rather, it comes with exposure, comfort level, motivation, familiarity, and practice in real communicative contexts. (Delpit 1995)

and hear clearly that a lot of thinking is happening and kids are very engaged.

We have many different levels of English speaking and many different personalities in our classrooms. Some feel totally comfortable speaking out; others may not. To address this we constantly try to provide opportunities for those kids to talk, whether in smaller groups, with us individually, or through expressing themselves in other ways, such as drawing or writing. Just because the kids aren't talking doesn't mean they aren't engaged in conversation. Conversation is also about the words surrounding you and what you take in; it isn't just about what you say aloud.

The more work we do with oral language, the easier it is for the kids to leap into texts. This work also needs to be in context and meaningful, and not random, rote memorization of grammar and vocabulary.

A group of emergent speakers wants desperately to learn about volcanoes during our unit on Japan. We search for books in their native language and are able to come up with a few so that instead of giving up or limiting their inquiry, we begin working on vocabulary about volcanoes in English. We use images of volcanoes exploding and talk about the nouns, adjectives, and verbs that bring the pictures to life: *hot, red, molten, lava, fire spits, ash blows, rocks fly, flows,* and many, many more. These intense words act as stepping-stones to the next level, which is labeling drawings the kids have made of their own volcanoes, followed by constructing sentences with standard grammar using conjunctive phrases, which leads to read-alouds of books on volcanoes, videos with powerful images, and discussions about where the lava comes from. The talk without follow-up, without connections being made to text and images, could easily have been lost, but because we chart vocabulary and parts of speech, talk about sounds and words, do write-alouds and read-alouds specific to the topic, make word walls that include not only vocabulary but short sentences with symbolic representations, use language structure/sentence frames, and take notes, what happens is an explosion of thought and interaction between the child and the English language.

Language acquisition progresses with every risk taken because exposure to new language structures increases. It is like a game, with each word being a toy. The more children play with their new language, the more at ease they are with it and the less overwhelming it becomes.

Now we bring the kids in close to the easel when we are having a mini-lesson and empower them with the possibility of choices and making decisions in their learning. With ELLs we want to show our confidence in them even at an early age. Our trust in them leads to motivation and excitement when we are exploring our curriculum. We also find that kids can focus more on their thinking, whether they are reading or writing, when they are given independence. With more than twenty first graders in one small room, it can at times be hard, but why shouldn't they be comfortable and have a choice?

We have had to let go of our fears and the desire to control and let the kids work outside, in the nooks and crannies, on the floor, and even in each other's rooms and trust that they can do it. Sometimes panic sets in and we find ourselves cruising around not believing the kids are doing what we expect, only to find that they are deeply involved in their work.

Kids Love to Be the Teacher—Let Them Facilitate

We like to get the ELLs involved in teaching other kids right away. We like the idea of a facilitator—someone who guides the lesson. To start, the kids act as facilitators when they share their writing. (See Figure 2.4.) They read their pieces and ask for responses from the class by saying, "Do you have any questions, comments, or connections?" We have modeled this again and again, which is how they know what to do. Later we take the facilitator role into book clubs, shared writings, and published pieces. The more the kids practice teaching and talking with the group, the more ownership they have of their learning and the more easily conversation flows. A lot of times the kids want to facilitate a read-aloud, so we let them.

One morning Alma pulled out Ezra Jack Keats's *A Snowy Day,* because it reminded her of the weather that morning. "Can I read to the class?" she asked.

"Go ahead. Sit in the meeting area and start."

FIGURE 2.4
Anain shares her research on mountains in Spanish.

"I have a story I want to read to you," she said in a loud voice. Heads popped up. She began *A Snowy Day*. We gently nudged the kids her way. She was on the second page by the time everyone wandered over. They sat and listened. When she had finished, she asked, "Does anyone have any questions or comments?" Thumbs went up. This was totally unplanned, but she seized the moment.

Teaching for Enhanced Learning

One technique that has been very successful for us is the use of sheltered instruction. Sheltered instruction is a way to deliver material so that it is comprehensible to all levels of ELLs and at the same time interesting and challenging for those students who speak English as their native language. We have heard from many people that they think sheltered instruction is "dumbing down" the curriculum. For us it is just the opposite. It is "enhanced learning," which is what we started calling it in a class discussion at the University of Colorado at Denver. To help us plan we often use a tool called the SIOP (Sheltered Instruction Observation Protocol) (Echevarria, Vogt, and Short 2000), which helps us design our lessons and adjust our teaching to meet the needs of all the kids in our class. We see sheltered instruction as a way to make the curriculum more exciting, and as a way to tap more deeply into the ideas that are being explored. For us it includes the following:

Use exciting and vibrant images.
Assess each and every child based on that child's needs.
Use gestures.
Pair visuals with text.
Use clear and precise speech.
Share writing.
Draw symbolic representations while speaking.
Categorize information using graphic organizers.
Label visuals and drawings.
Encourage active hands-on learning.
Arrange field trips connected to content and reinforced before and
     after the actual trip.
Use vocabulary in context.
Contextualize learning/integrated thematic units.
Model mistakes to encourage approximations and to have ways to get
     unstuck.
Document activities with a digital camera.

Foster vocabulary development using preview/review. (Using pictures that are connected to the vocabulary, preview the key vocabulary before beginning a lesson and then review it at the conclusion of the lesson.)

Clearly state purpose.

Use guarded vocabulary (minimize the use of colloquial language).

Use realia (real life objects).

Enthusiasm, Engagement, Intensity, and Momentum

Maintaining day-to-day momentum has been critical to keeping the energy and drive in students' research and thinking. From day to day it is very important to capitalize on the excitement from the research. Imagine being able to think, read, and write about your topic that you want to explore, but being given only thirty minutes twice a week to do it. Probably not a lot of exploration or learning is going to take place, but if you are given an hour or more a day to examine your learning interests, a deeper level of learning will likely occur. When an idea is fresh in a child's mind, she is excited and can generate more questions and ideas from what she is writing about. If the child puts a piece of work away for too long, that momentum and all that intense interest can be lost. This is part of the practice of writing—consistency in the amount of time and energy put into a project.

Continuity and Momentum

Act as a scribe to get their thinking immediately into text.

Leave the kids' work out as "thinking in progress."

Use repetitive daily writing routines.

Have kids choose what they want to write about and what they know.

Allow sufficient time for writing.

Celebrate work through publishing, displaying, presenting, and writing.

Model new routines until students internalize them.

Take thinking tours.

Use children's life experiences as stepping-stones.

Remember that the kids' art can stand alone as meaning making.

Tristian has returned from a trip to New Mexico. At a rest stop she had the opportunity to see the landscape close up. She noticed things that sparked her curiosity. She noticed a lone tree in the distance, spiders crawling on bushes nearby, and a big deep blue sky. When she gets back to class she immediately begins a narrative based on her recent experience. Next she decides she wants to know more about the desert, so off she goes to the school library, where she gathers a handful of books and magazines. Tristian takes a note-taking sheet out and begins to write down what interests her. She is most curious about the plants and animals. She reads text and looks at the images. She writes.

Tristian's story about her trip is about one page long. She has used the word wall and words from print around the room to help her spell. Words she doesn't know she gets down by thinking about what the beginning, middle, and ending sounds might be, then circling them. She knows we can come back and fix them, but the most important thing now is to get her thoughts down. She writes about how she saw animal footprints in the sand and wonders what animal made them. From her inquiry we will soon explore more about the desert. When she is finished, she reads it out loud. We edit and confer. She hadn't capitalized the *n* in *New* or the *m* in *Mexico*. We say to her, "You know what? People who read this will expect you to capitalize those letters because it's a name and we do that with names." She agrees. This process takes a few days until she thinks she is ready to publish.

We take strips of white paper to put her notes into sentences. We write (on sticky notes) as Tristian puts her notes into sentences, therefore editing along the way. She copies her words onto the strips of paper. Tristian then adds images to her text. She organizes her images and text for publishing, glues them down, and reads and explains her thinking to the class. As her piece hangs in the classroom, kids read it and write comments on sticky notes. This initial inquiry leads Tristian to her next project, the desert.

A PERSONAL REFLECTION

Thinking about changing the way we taught was difficult for both of us. We had our own ideas about the way things should be and felt pressures from others. It isn't easy to try something new, to rearrange a room to fit the needs of others, to rethink and relearn ways of interacting with students, but this has been a wonderful learning process. Although it was scary and we are often bombarded with doubts and questions, we have seen that it creates a community of thinkers who are eager to wonder and learn about their world and each other.

CHAPTER THREE

TELLING OUR STORIES

We read our world. We write our words. We read our words. This is how the kids start writing. The kids know themselves and their world better than anything, and by working on personal narratives it is easy for them to get their thinking down on paper and to read their own writing, because it is part of their schema. Our goal is for them to acquire dispositions of writers so they have the desire and ability to get their thoughts down. For our students the best place to start has been having them write what they know about, or are interested in.

Ultimately every writer must follow the path that feels most comfortable. For most people learning to write, that path is nonfiction. It enables them to write about what they know or can observe or can find out. This is especially true of young people and students. They will write far more willingly about situations that have reality—experiences that touch their own lives—or subjects they have an aptitude for. (Zinsser 1998)

There are unlimited ways in which ELLs learn to express themselves through writing. The key is to make it fun and exciting and allow for discovery along the way.

KEEPING OUR STORIES ALIVE

FIGURE 3.1
The kids share their daily lives through "Second-Grade News."

Part of what we do to learn about each other is encourage the telling of stories about ourselves. Both teachers and kids share stories from day one. We do this a number of different ways, and we begin the journey within the supportive structure of shared reading and writing. Shared writing is an excellent way for ELLs to practice language structures orally and see conventional grammar and syntax modeled. We have been using a format called Class News. As a class we create daily news almost every day from day one. This routine allows the kids to contribute to a writing, reading, listening, and speaking activity that is all about them. (See Figure 3.1.)

Often we write our news early in the morning and find it a good way to start the day. First we write the title of our news, for example, "First-Grade News" or "Second-Grade News" or something more exciting such as "The Class Adventures for [date]." We ask the kids to think about what news we have that we can write. After giving them a couple of minutes of quiet time to think, we let them tell someone next to them what they are thinking. Next, as we hold the pen we ask someone to share. Often they like to start with the weather. For example, "Today is hot and sunny." We first draw lines to represent where words will go, usually using a yellow or light-colored marker. Drawing lines for each word emphasizes spaces for words and makes a connection between voice and print. Then we ask, "What goes at the beginning of a sentence?" We choose someone who has a thumb up. As we write, we stop sometimes to talk about letter sounds, coloring in some of the letters. For a word such as *Thursday* we would talk about the beginning sound and color in the *th* to make it stand out—a brief graphophonic lesson.

> ### BENEFITS FOR ELLS
>
> #### Shared Writing Experiences
> ✓ Shared writing and reading provides a less stressful environment for risk taking.
> ✓ Class news is in their world and their words.
> ✓ Conventions are talked about every day with class news.
> ✓ It provides more text for the kids to read on a regular basis.
> ✓ It is another way for ELLs to expand and practice vocabulary.
> ✓ It helps ELLs see conventional grammatical structures in their new language.
> ✓ It allows ELLs to see their words turned into print in an authentic way.

We also stop before the end of a sentence and ask, "What is the next word?" This gives the kids practice with semantic cues. They need to put in a word that makes sense. When we come to the end of the sentence, we ask, "What do writers put at the end of a sentence?" Sometimes we say, "Tell someone next to you what goes at the end of a sentence." This gives everyone a chance to talk, and we write what they say. With this shared writing we are able to teach in-context conventions, English syntax, vocabulary, graphophonics, semantic cues, and more. We also point out differences and similarities between English and Spanish, such as cognates and letter sounds, as a way to show the students the relationships between the two, because we have a large number of Spanish-speaking students. Each day we choose a couple of colors such as blue and green and alternate colors for each sentence. We also draw small pictures to represent some of the words. In the sentence "Today is hot and sunny," we might draw a sun above the word *sunny* and a thermometer above *hot*. The pictures help make the text more comprehensible to our new English learners. When we are finished, we take turns reading our news together. In twenty minutes we have already written and read a newspaper!

BRINGING STORIES TO LIFE THROUGH WRITER'S WORKSHOP

Writer's workshop is a time when the kids can share their thinking and let it explode into a book, poster, mobile, or anything else they might want to create.

The heart and soul of the kids' writing has been watching them bring their stories to life, which goes hand in hand with our belief that by honoring their thinking we allow them to show what they know. Each and every child has a special and different story to tell, which, as they write them down, fills our classrooms with new background knowledge and reveals who they are. These personal narratives are stepping-stones to inquiry.

Their Own Ideas

At the beginning and throughout the year we focus on ideas with our ELLs. This has been an important first step in encouraging them to get their thinking on paper. It has also helped us to get to know them. When children are free to draw or write whatever they want, a certain depth in their personalities is revealed. It is also a positive way to introduce initial steps of the writing process. Emergent ELLs can express their thinking both orally and through drawings, much like emergent native speakers. By focusing on ideas and acting as scribes we are providing our ELLs with two very important pieces of the writing process. For us, ideas come first and mechanics second. The more our ELLs focus on ideas, the more they write, and the mechanics come with editing, conferring, and publishing. We don't want to stifle their thinking, and thus we work with them to get ideas down on paper. We are able to model conventional writing, and the kids see their work on the printed page.

In our big picture we want the kids to be independent thinkers and to release them to explore their inquiries and interests on their own. We try to help them with cultural capital in that they know people in our society expect conventions in place in their writing. They know it's important, but they know their ideas are also valued. As Stephen Krashen says, "The purpose of language instruction is to provide students with what they need to know so they can progress without us" (2003).

Every child has a writer's notebook, which can be any kind of notebook that feels comfortable in their hands. We provide them with a variety, such as tiny composition books, spiral-bound notebooks, journals, bound books with blank pages, whatever they like to use to get their thoughts down. We don't like to limit them in this because we don't want it to seem as though we are trying to control their creativity. Some folks are unnerved by such a wide variety of choices, but for us it's not a big deal because we work on management routines so much that the kids become responsible for their own stuff. They keep their writing with their books in their book boxes, which for us is logical because it is another resource for them to use to read and gather information. Keeping track is easy.

The kids start by writing their personal narratives in their journals. They can write about anything they want, and usually do. Their journal/writing notebook is a place to express their thinking in a low-risk environment. They know that it is just the starting point for their writing. Once we have conferred with them and talked about how to add more details to their writing, to remember why we use capitals and periods, we help them move from their notebooks to a large sheet of chart paper. At first we draw lines to help them approximate where to write on the page and how to use all of the space; after doing it several times they know how to do it alone. They use their artistic expertise to draw, paint, and color their narratives. When they are finished, they share their thinking and get responses from their peers both orally and in writing. Their stories about cats, a day on the playground, a butterfly, their sister, or anything else suddenly comes alive for all to see and read.

Drawing gives me ideas to write. If I draw a cat, it gives me ideas (to write) for some reason. I used to have a cat.
—*Michael*

Stephanie loves to write about her little sister. She scribbles away in her notebook about how they play Barbies, watch movies, and eat pizza on the weekend. As she writes, she circles words she isn't sure how to spell, knowing that during conferencing and revision she can come back and edit them. This way her thoughts aren't stifled and she can keep the flow of her writing going. When she finishes, she begins a drawing, filling it with color and including exquisite detail. Adding art is something she has internalized as part of the writing process. She is connecting the drawing with her words and vice versa. Whereas Stephanie chooses to write first and then draw, other kids draw first and find words in their drawings. Later, when she publishes on chart paper, the drawings will be different, but she still takes the time now to make them as beautiful as the ones in her published version.

Eric Carle once said, "Sometimes I draw first then I write." So we let kids draw first, too. This is something we were reluctant to do, probably because we thought we needed to keep the kids more accountable through the written word. We know their art and illustrations are thinking that is significant, and maybe the underlying stress of the state tests looming over us caused us not to follow our hearts initially. Now we are more conscious that their art is a major part of their thinking and we let them do that first if they want to. Although emergent ELLs may have trouble getting their thoughts in writing in conventional English, they often are able to express their thinking through drawings, paintings, collages, and many other artistic media. Sometimes it seems they are just bursting inside to get some markers or paint in their hands and start drawing. This enthusiasm for a topic they are interested in leads to wondering, reading, writing, and more reading.

Art as Meaning Making

Drawing is also a medium through which the kids are developing questions and making discoveries about certain things. For example, during our unit on insects Jaime is diligently examining a diagram of an ant. He wants to draw it as big as he can so he can put labels on the parts of the body.

"Anne, Anne!" he shouts out excitedly.

"What, Jaime?"

"Ants are poisonous."

"Are you sure?" she asks, thinking that he has somehow misread something.

"Look, here it says 'venom sack.'" As clear as day on the page the label identifies a small pouch at the back of the ant as a venom sack. Anne isn't sure about this so they hop on the Internet to check some on-line resources. Their search results in the answer. Ants do have a harmless venom, which is why it stings when they bite.

"We both learned something today, Jaime. Thanks!" Anne says. It was through his drawing that Jaime had discovered and shared information that he otherwise may have not found.

Stories Written and Illustrated on Chart Paper

Before Stephanie launches into publishing on chart paper, we sit down to confer and notice the circled words. It is during these times with the kids that we are able to see their approximations with syntax, word choice, and style, which helps us plan future instruction. We work with her to revise the story about her sister until she is happy with it. We practice using strategies such as accessing different kinds of texts to look for vocabulary (dictionaries, thesauruses, other books, word walls). We also make it clear that there are writing conventions that she will be expected to use so that she begins to develop the knowledge, attitude, and desire of a writer who has the cultural capital to write for different kinds of audiences and use different kinds of registers. (See Figure 3.2.)

Let Her Be

"Mabel, we need you to come over and join us, please." It's early October, and we are getting together to do a shared write, an edition of "First-Grade News." Mabel, sitting not too far from us, does not look up, and continues cutting out her fabric. For her, this is a big step, because she has spent the majority of the first couple of months of school crying, huddled under a table, or trying to escape into the hallways to wander the building. Everyone in the school knows who she is and helps us keep an eye on her. Today, though, she is totally engaged in her poster. Spread out in front of her are scissors, glue, a piece of computer paper, a small pile of fabric pieces, and a

FIGURE 3.2
Cloe writes about her new baby brother and her mother being pregnant.

box of colorful markers. Mabel is teaching us about what it means to comply with teacher requests to make us "happy," because she clearly is not interested in what the group is doing. Again, we try. "Mabel, we would love to have you come over and write with us. Just leave your art out and you can finish later." Same response. Mabel is focused on what she is doing—cutting out shapes of fabric to make an illustration of a doll. We decide to let her be because she is so engaged in what she is doing at the moment.

After twenty minutes we finish our shared writing and the kids are released to read and write. Mabel calls some of us over and shares with those of us who are curious about what she has created. Triangles, squares, and other shapes of fabric bring her doll to life on the paper. She had an idea and wanted to demonstrate a different way to make meaning, that is, through her art. This time, in this place, we let her be and trusted her to work on what mattered to her. Our fear has us hearing a million voices in our heads. "She needs to be held accountable. What message does this send to the rest of the class? She can do whatever she wants? Is she listening? Is it a power struggle? What should we do?" Our answer is to let her be and help her move to the next stage. We could leave her doll as it is on her paper, but we decide to ask if she would like to write a short story about it. Mabel, an emergent ELL reader and writer, quietly says, "Yes." Knowing that we need to seize the moment, we waste no time in getting Mabel's story written and published. We plop down a large pad of paper and grab a pencil, a thick black marker, and her newly created doll. Kneeling on the floor with a pencil in hand we ask Mabel, "What do you want to call your story? Do you want to write a title first?"

"I want to call it 'Dolls,'" she says. With the pencil we lightly write what she wants for her title. As we write the letters, we talk about how we form them.

"Capital *D* is tall stick down, up, and backward *C*. *O* is around, right? *L* is tall stick down, over, and *S* is *C*, backward *C*. Since we've written the title, people will want to know who illustrated and wrote this." We continue, to keep her going, "Story and pictures by . . ."

Then she jumps in. "Story and pictures by Mabel." Again with the pencil we lightly write. To get this far has taken us about fifteen minutes. Now we get to her story.

"What do you want people to know about this?" we ask. Mabel takes her time and thinks. Nothing comes out. We decide to press on a bit. "What is this colorful art you made?"

"I made a doll."

"Do you want to write that?" we ask. She nods. With the pencil in our hand and black marker in hers, we continue. "How do people expect us to begin a sentence?"

"A capital letter," she replies.

"You know how to end a sentence, so you can do that yourself." As she goes over her words with black marker, we get up and move around to the other kids doing similar things, then make our way back to Mabel. We have found that it is often important to sit with the kids in these earlier stages and keep them going. Letting go of trying to do everything and be everywhere all at once is something we have also learned. Through Mabel's story we have had a conversation about her world and incorporated what writers do to take their thinking public. Mabel's story is now this:

Dolls
Written and illustrated by Mabel
I made a doll.
I like to make dolls.
I made it with fabric and glue!

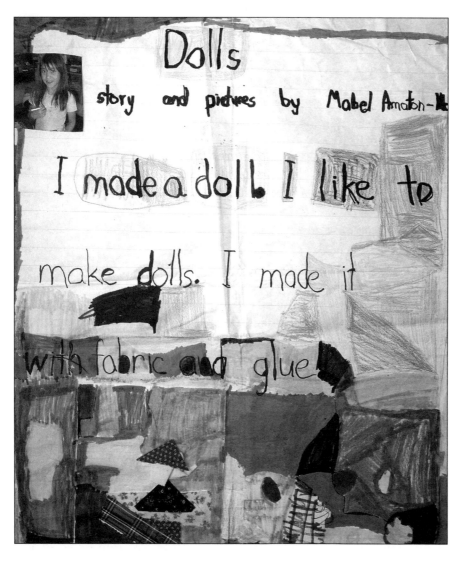

FIGURE 3.3
Mabel meticulously created this
poster about dolls using markers,
fabric, and paints.

We know this is a stepping-stone for her further development as a thinker and writer. She will spend the next couple of days completing her illustrations around her original fabric doll. A comment sheet, an "About Me" section, and her dedication, are added later.

Occasionally some of the kids have times like Mabel when they want to be in their own space even though they are just a few feet away. With her story about dolls Mabel helped teach us how to honor those times and feelings. (See Figure 3.3.)

Scribing

As a step toward independent writing, we work with our ELLs to get their thinking down by scribing. Scribing, or writing what the kids say on strips of

BENEFITS FOR ELLS

Scribing

✓ Their writing is used as valid classroom text.

✓ Kids are able to approximate their new language.

✓ Kids can see that what they say can be written.

✓ It provides a low-stress way to begin writing.

✓ Their identity becomes visible.

✓ Success is guaranteed.

paper, is a good scaffold for ELLs, drawing a line under each word. This is great way for them to internalize writing conventions. By drawing lines for emergent writers we help them practice spacing, let them know exactly how many words are in each sentence, and show them where the punctuation goes. Early on, writing requires a lot of labor on their part because their motor skills are developing. The kids are seeing that what they say can be written into words, and that those words are important enough to be written down and read. As they talk, we scribe. We also use the computer to scribe what they are saying. Often the images they have drawn in their writer's notebooks tell in-depth stories of their lives and they are able to share them orally while we help them get the words into print.

After we write some of their thinking down, maybe four to eight sentences, we ask them how they want to show their thinking. It could be as a poster or even as a book. What's the title? We write it down. Who is this for? We need a dedication. Whose thinking is this? We need to write who did the writing and illustrating. We write their thinking down on sentence strips, sticky notes, or even in their notebooks. With the writing spread out, we play around with where we want to put the words. Do we want them all in one place or should we spread them out so there is room for illustrations? We draw lines precisely the same way as the scribed sheet. That way the kids have a duplicate and can write their words more easily. It also allows them to practice using their visual memory.

We Write and Read Our Own Books

At the beginning of first grade Yok is an emergent speaker of English and communicates in writing primarily through pictures. Instead of stopping at the pictures, however, we are able to promote the written word through a series of questions and comments, through oral language, and through observation of his drawings. It is a great way to get to know him and to begin work with him in our new classroom.

"Yok, let's put some words to your pictures."

"Okay!"

"The computer, sticky notes, or sentence strips?"

"Computer!" We sit down with his notebook open to his drawings and begin typing on the computer. We find we can get the momentum going if the kids feel successful right away. Writing can be very time consuming and labor intensive for these little guys. Kids get frustrated and tired from always holding the pen themselves. It's enjoyable for them to take a break once in a while and get their thinking down faster.

FIGURE 3.4
The kids write books about their lives
and personal experiences.

"Tell me what's happening here." As always, amazement creeps in when we realize how much of a story there is to the kids' art. Every little scribble or doodle has a reason behind it, and there is a story behind each drawing. Together we begin with a title that Yok dictates. He decides to call his new piece "Jets."

"Who is the author of 'Jets'?"

"Me!" He spells out his first and last names.

"Now other people will know who wrote it," we say. We continue together, writing the date and a dedication. "Who is this information for?" Yok decides to dedicate this work to his family. He shares the information in his own words. A dedication helps writers establish a purpose and an audience as well as personalize and take ownership of their work. (See Figure 3.4.)

As we scribe student stories using the computer, we have found it important to say, "Watch me. These are your words I'm writing. Do you see how what you say can be written down for other people to read?" The kids talk. We type. "This is where a lot of writers write," we say. Yok talks about the different kinds of jets he knows about. He points to his jet drawings and tells us about them. Some of the jets are flying to different places, and some are at the airport getting fuel and cargo.

For Yok, writing about something he is interested in and already knows about is much easier and more fun than writing about something he knows little or nothing about. As he talks through his drawings, he is seeing his words written down in conventional structures. The more we write like this together, the sooner he will internalize the process and begin to write more independently. We make the font bold and larger than 12 points to allow for easier reading. Each page we write has one or two sentences, which gives some space for illustrations. Yok's book has four pages with a

FIGURE 3.5
Yok's smile about his new book tells
it all.

total of seven sentences. Now we talk about how we should reread what we've written and see if it looks all right or decide whether to add or change anything. We tell him that this is what writers do so they know their words make sense. The end of his book has a little section with the title "About Me." In the beginning we have a frame: "I like to _____. I also like to _____. My favorite thing to do is _____." The frame helps them formulate and internalize the structure for their "About Me" paragraph. Finally, we write a comment sheet that says, "Please write your questions, comments, and connections here."

Yok takes one of his copies and places it in his backpack to illustrate at home. Through this process we are individually conferring with him. Through our conversation while sitting at the computer, we can help him experience the process of writing and how it can be fun. As Yok is illustrating, other kids take interest in what he is doing, which leads Yok to read his book to them. Later when Yok has finished his illustrating he is ready to share. We start reading the book as a signal to bring the class to our meeting area. The kids walk over and sit down, some having conversations along the way, but settling in and listening after a few minutes. We continue to read a few pages, then stop to announce Yok's published book, which creates a large smile. (See Figure 3.5.)

By reading aloud we are modeling what it looks like to share. We make sure we point to the images while reading so everyone can see. Now it's Yok's turn. He begins with his title and dedication and continues to read and discuss his illustrations. He finishes with "About Me" and then asks, "What questions, comments, or connections do you have?" First we do this orally and the teacher writes the comments. We like to give the kids positive reinforcement by telling them what we like about their story and writing it down for everyone to see. In each student book we have a page or two in the back titled "Please write your questions and comments here." We date our comments so that the kids can track them and see who is reading their work and when.

Eventually we get out some sticky notes so students can write on them and stick them in Yok's book. Often they write, "I love your story," which is what they did for Yok's. Some of them even draw images of what they are thinking, like a jet zooming over the earth. They know how to do this because we have practiced by using sentence frames such as, "I love your story because _____." Now the first-time author and ELL has shared and gotten instant feedback on his thinking from his peers. The next day when we are writing, Yok is still drawing pictures, but he has experienced success and is clearly motivated. Soon he will be writing the words for his pictures on his own.

This is how we get going early in the year. The new speakers of English are seeing themselves as risk takers, and they see that writing can be fun, especially when you get to draw and share your thinking. Yok, for example, is able to approximate new language structures and doesn't have to worry about decoding words in isolation or out of context to function. His English language output doesn't have to interfere with him making his thinking visible. Instead of being dependent on the teacher the kids become more motivated and excited about writing. They also are in the process of internalizing what writing and publishing looks like.

> ### BENEFITS FOR ELLS
>
> #### Personal Narratives
>
> ✓ It develops grammatical structures and vocabulary that is relevant to their world.
>
> ✓ It establishes a community of learners where children share information with one another and respect one another.
>
> ✓ Scribing is a contextual thinking routine (it's their story and their words).
>
> ✓ Books provide opportunities for others to read and respond.

Learning to Trust

Trust is a big factor in making this work. Often kids are spread out in the circle area, markers, paper, glue, paint, and glitter scattered about. Conversations are plentiful. We notice them moving back and forth in their conversations about the topics they are investigating and their personal lives. We sit on the floor and listen in. We watch to see who needs help. We are there to sometimes guide the conversation back to their topics if need be—a sort of refocusing. We are there to give them ideas about how to make their thinking become more alive, to add to their repertoire. We also move to the other areas of the room where kids are writing and reading together. We notice, too, that sometimes the kids need a nudge—maybe to add more illustrations, or to add part of the text structure that is missing (for example, where they found their information). Getting all this to work takes a lot of thought on our part. We need to be prepared with a lot of materials. We need to be energized, and when we see what the kids have to say in their words and their illustrations, we are!

Taking Ownership Affects Their Writing

Without ownership the kids' life in school is all a blank whiteboard. Ownership is huge for all writers, but even more so for children acquiring another language because of the deep connections they make between their

I'm going to make another poster about books. It will be a poem. It will say books have sweet pages that say sweet words!—Cloe

work and their peers, their native language and their new language, themselves and their teachers. So often children who are acquiring English feel alone and like they are living in silence, particularly in the early stages of acquisition. If they can take ownership of their work, it is that much easier and more fun for them to make connections with their schoolwork and the surrounding environment. Try to imagine feeling absolutely lost and alone. Imagine that everything around you is unfamiliar, that street signs make no sense, that menus in restaurants are foreign, that food tastes different, that music is strange, that your friends are no longer by your side, and you have been thrown into a situation where no one understands you and everyone seems frustrated by you. This is what it is like for a child who is a new speaker of English in a new country. If they can have one thing in the world that is just theirs, that they can take hold of and cherish even just for a moment, it could be the turning point that enables them to gain a level of comfort and begin to find their niche.

FIGURE 3.6
Cynthia writes a message to us on our classroom message board.

INTERACTIVE WRITING ABOUT OUR WORLD

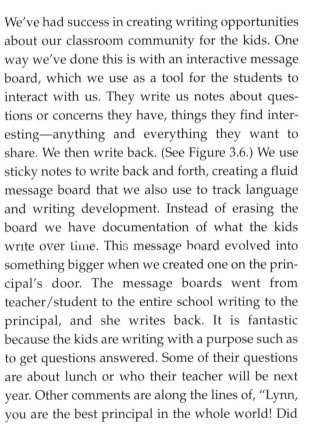

We've had success in creating writing opportunities about our classroom community for the kids. One way we've done this is with an interactive message board, which we use as a tool for the students to interact with us. They write us notes about questions or concerns they have, things they find interesting—anything and everything they want to share. We then write back. (See Figure 3.6.) We use sticky notes to write back and forth, creating a fluid message board that we also use to track language and writing development. Instead of erasing the board we have documentation of what the kids write over time. This message board evolved into something bigger when we created one on the principal's door. The message boards went from teacher/student to the entire school writing to the principal, and she writes back. It is fantastic because the kids are writing with a purpose such as to get questions answered. Some of their questions are about lunch or who their teacher will be next year. Other comments are along the lines of, "Lynn, you are the best principal in the whole world! Did

FIGURE 3.7
Miguel and Jaime write to Lynn, our principal, on the message board on her office door.

you know that?" A message like that from one of the kids gives us the energy to keep going. (See Figure 3.7.)

The message boards allow kids the opportunity to participate in volunteer literacy events such as reading, writing, and responding. These are voluntary because the kids choose to participate in them on their own.

Field Trips Generate New Experiences

Another way to create experiences is through field trips. They are wonderful resources, particularly if the kids initiate the writing. One spring we went to the IMAX Theater to see a film about coral reefs. On the bus ride home, Mabel, who always loads her bag with notebooks, sticky notes, pens, and markers, was hunched over in her seat, quieter than usual. A second look revealed that she was scribbling away in her notebook. "What are you writing?"

Her round saucer-shaped brown eyes looked up and she grinned. She held the notebook up and the title read "Great Barrier Reef." She was writing about the day's events. "Can I read it to you?" she asked, and she settled in with her notebook resting on her knees, which she had pulled up to her chest. As the bus bumped along toward home, Mabel wrote out of her own desire to make her thinking visible and share it with her community.

BENEFITS FOR ELLS

Writing Their World

✓ It creates a real-life writing routine.

✓ It allows for authentic writing and is a valuable way to communicate with each other.

✓ It increases opportunities for risk taking in writing.

✓ It means more time to use new vocabulary and language structures.

She had taken something that was part of her day and written about it, internalizing it and making it her own. This made us smile because it was a realization of the big picture. Mabel had the motivation, the will, the confidence, and the tools to share her world and words in English.

Snapping Photos

We also like to use pictures to tell a story. Using a digital camera to inspire ELLs to write stories about themselves or experiences they have had has been a wonderful tool for us. It has helped us solve the problem of getting the kids' work home. We take pictures all the time of them writing, reading, playing, on field trips, and performing in school plays. We save the pictures and print them out for the kids to use as a starting point for writing and reading stories about themselves. It helps refresh their memory about what they were doing at any given point, serves as an image from which to generate rich vocabulary, and can be used as part of the artwork in the final published piece. When the kids see themselves on paper, doing things they love, they become inspired to write and share those experiences. When Anne had her baby and e-mailed a picture of herself and her newborn, Joseito, Brad printed it out and glued it on a piece of construction paper. He left it out to see what would happen. After the excitement of looking at the new photo passed, Alina picked up a pen and sticky note and wrote, "Anne, I like your baby." The flood of messages followed as the kids gradually added their congratulations and even questions. When Anne returned from maternity leave, it was hanging on the classroom door. The writing was heartfelt, authentic text straight from the kids. (See Figure 3.8.)

Our kids are used to being photographed working and having their images posted on the classroom and school walls. They also see themselves working in slide shows we create on the computer. Capturing them on film surrounded by books, magazines, markers, paint, and other supplies helps give them a different perspective on what great things they are doing. We also print images of the kids and have them write captions on sticky notes and tape them to the walls for everyone to see and read. Parents stopping by love to see these snapshots of the day, too.

Using a camera also lets us include a picture of the author on kids' writing, which puts a face with the name. A seemingly little thing like that can do a lot to help us create an environment that enhances thinking dispositions. We see the kids' pride come out in their smiles when their work is put up. With small pictures attached to the posters the entire school audience of kids, parents, teachers, and visitors can see the faces responsible for this great thinking. It helps us realize our goal of getting the kids excited and enthusiastic about their writing and inquiries.

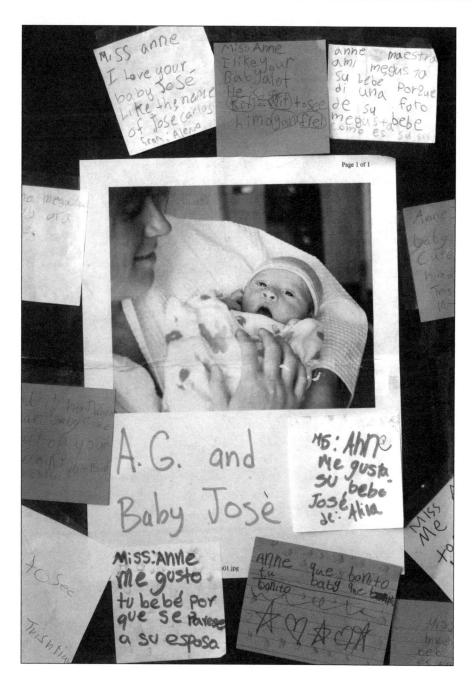

FIGURE 3.8
The kids write notes to Anne after
Joseito is born.

A PERSONAL REFLECTION

Letting go and allowing the kids to write what they want to write about has
been difficult. It is challenging to weave curriculum into the writing and still
let the kids follow their hearts. As we work toward creating a culture of

thinking and learning and as we go through the process of learning how to work with culturally and linguistically diverse (CLD) students, we try to keep in mind something that Sonia Nieto said: "Culture is not static; nor is it necessarily positive or negative" (2000). The idea that culture is not static goes directly to the core of our teaching. It means that we must use each other and other members of the greater community as resources. It also means that we have to agree on this when working together and be flexible enough to work through the ideas and difficulties that arise when working within a system that has not historically supported transformational teaching. We have to admit that we don't know everything and that we must listen to the kids and their families to continue making our culture of thinking and learning pertinent and relevant to their lives.

CHAPTER FOUR

LAUNCHING READERS

Because of the writing our kids are doing, including publishing and illustrating, some people wonder where we fit reading into the day. Just to make it clear, we do believe that the more we read, the better writers we will be and vice versa. To promote books of all genres we incorporate a gradual-release-of-responsibility framework (Pearson et al. 1992) through read-alouds, shared readings, reading conferences, and independent reading. The goal is to expose the kids to a variety of writing structures, new vocabulary, how punctuation is used, and how books are organized.

We want the kids to be exploring all the great nonfiction informational texts, so we teach them to read, doing our best to get them enthusiastic about reading. We explicitly teach reading strategies for both decoding and comprehending text so they can better access books, magazines, and posters. In the process of reading all these great nonfiction books we make sure to focus on their many nonfiction features. Once the kids are surrounded by a lot of nonfiction books that contain inspiring images, they can't help but pick them up and start browsing, wondering, and noticing. We start on this the first day of school.

One of our fundamental principles is to foster a love of books and reading. We also think that the higher the quality and accessibility of the texts we surround the kids with, the more likely they will be to pick them up and start reading the words. ELLs really respond to high-quality images, and even if they can't read the text, the images are accessible to them. The reality is, though, that we are nowhere near satisfied with the number of books we have. Many of the books we've acquired were discarded by other teachers, the library, and the district. We look through these discards and see if there is anything that is still relevant. If it's not relevant, we don't use it. As we get new modern books, which is always a happy day, we replace those that are out of date or lacking the kinds of vibrant images and interesting text we strive for in our classrooms.

One solution we have come up with is to cut apart books and make posters or study prints out of them. It's easy. We take two copies of the same book, cut the pages apart, and laminate them so that we have two pages on one large sheet of construction paper. We hang it on the board so the kids can easily see us modeling. We write on it, read, and then we let the kids use them, practicing reading or note taking. With cut-apart books the kids can choose to focus on one or two pages of the book rather than many pages, so the amount of information isn't so overwhelming. It also means that several children can read the same book at the same time and share the pages. The cut-apart books are taken page by page by each of the kids to look at and read. We all know that reading aloud is like advertising a book. Modeling with a cut-up book is the same thing. Often after a mini-lesson a lot of the kids want to take the very page we were modeling with to read and write on their own.

CHOOSING TEXTS

When thinking about ELLs we constantly need to provide access to meaningful print, which is part of the space in a room. The more background knowledge an ELL student has, the more advanced level of text she can comprehend. A more beginning-level book for which a child has no background knowledge may be less comprehensible for an ELL, which is something to think about when helping children choose books. Taking the time to sit with them and talk about what topics and themes interest them helps us help them find books that motivate them to read.

Read-Alouds

Although we know read-alouds are important for all emergent readers and writers, they are particularly helpful for ELLs. We often read stories three and four times within relatively short periods of time to explore language and thought. This repetition once again gives ELLs access to their new language and text through pictures and modeling of conventional English. It allows them to develop their listening and speaking skills with texts that become more familiar to them with each read. With kids who have more experience, reading and rereading allows a deeper look at the story.

We begin by reading and rereading many narrative picture books in August and September and keep going throughout the year. Narrative picture books allow us to begin with some kids and continue with others our conversations about what thoughtful readers do. Whereas we get new arrivals from outside the United States, other kids will be coming from a kindergarten class that has had many conversations about reading comprehension strategies. We read aloud with many things in mind. With our ELLs we want to increase comprehension by slowing down and really articulating our words when reading. Pointing to the images and making gestures when appropriate to enhance new vocabulary helps kids make sense of what we are reading. We also carefully choose our books so that they are linked to the content. This is what integrated thematic units are about. We have spent significant time and money investing in literature that is linked to content so that we can make connections between what we study and the books we read.

Features of Nonfiction Texts

We spend considerable amounts of time reading all sorts of nonfiction texts to expose the kids to many different kinds before beginning to delve more deeply into them. Often these texts are directly related to our content units; other times they are connected to the inquiries the kids are interested in. As we begin to explore these texts more deeply, we begin to share with the kids

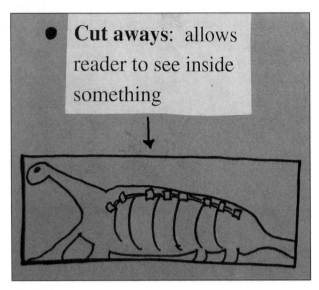

FIGURE 4.1
We create nonfiction feature posters with the kids and post them in our rooms.

the different features of nonfiction texts (Harvey and Goudvis 2000). We look at features such as labels, captions, cutaways, close-ups, comparisons, types of print, maps, scale diagrams, tables of contents, glossaries, indexes, appendices, and bibliographies. We start by examining which features to teach and then begin creating an anchor chart.

Anytime we are reading or the kids choose to read informational texts, we point out features as we come across them. After the first month of school we begin to introduce nonfiction features through lessons. With large pieces of construction paper we make nonfiction feature posters. (See Figure 4.1.) Each sheet of construction paper has one feature on it, and we create them together. On each poster we have the nonfiction feature, what it is, and an image of what it might look like. Introducing one nonfiction feature every few days works well for the kids. In this way we take our time and have fun exploring, and no one gets overwhelmed by too much information.

To practice locating the different features we do the following:

- Post the objective
- Gather nonfiction books and magazines with great images that emphasize the targeted features
- Have a discussion about what we are looking for and model
- Use sticky notes and pens to track our thinking
- Do a think-pair-share
- Release the kids to explore

The Language of Nonfiction

The vocabulary the kids need to access the texts has to be explicitly introduced and taught. We do mini-lessons around the different features to get them more familiar with the language of nonfiction texts. An easy one to start with is captions. The kids are gathered close, our poster is taped to an easel, and the topic of the mini-lesson is written above it: "We are learning about nonfiction features. Today we are learning about captions." Next we have a discussion of what captions are; they give us information about an image or picture. Anytime we say the word *caption,* we point to it and the image on the poster. By pointing we are linking text and images with what we are saying, making what we are saying more comprehensible. Next we quickly model what the kids are going to do. "Watch us, because you are going to do this in a couple of minutes." Taking some sticky notes, a pen, and some nonfiction books we have in front of us, we model exploring them for captions. When we come across one, we read it and look at the image. Grabbing a sticky note, we write the caption on it and stick it in the book. Now we turn it back over to the kids. As with other lessons we ask them, "What did you see us doing? Let's take a minute and think." As they are thinking, we write the sentence frame "I saw you _____." After a minute of silence we have the kids share with each other what they saw us doing. As they talk, we listen in and write what they say. Later as an assessment we play a game called "Find That Text Feature." We have the kids find as many features as they can in a text and chart them as a class. For example, if five kids find captions, eight find labels, and ten find an index, we tally them up and graph them. This is just a variation to keep us thinking about the text features. There are no winners or losers; we all work together.

Some of the things kids say are "I saw you reading captions," or "I saw you writing the word *caption* on your sticky note," or "I saw you looking at the picture and thinking." After a few more responses we know everyone knows what to do. With our eyes we let them go one by one to search for captions. On their way they choose some books that are spread out on the floor, sticky notes, and a pen. After the last student gets his or her supplies, we get up and confer with the kids. They draw a picture of what they find and add text to it, either labeling or writing complete sentences. After about fifteen minutes of exploring the books we regroup and share what we have found. We put the sticky notes on a chart for everyone to see. After each feature is taught and explored, we put our nonfiction feature poster up where everyone can see it. We move through the different features over the course of the year and constantly revisit them by pointing them out when we or the kids come across them. The kids begin applying them to their own work as they become more comfortable. (See Figure 4.2.) We

FIGURE 4.2
Lupita draws and labels the egg laid by a caterpillar on her poster about butterflies.

encourage our student nonfiction writers to do what a lot of books for kids don't, which is to attach images that are directly related to the text. The kids use nonfiction features that we've talked about earlier such as underlining important words, printing in bold letters or highlighting important text or vocabulary, labeling their pictures, and writing captions. Doing these things helps the students not only comprehend the vocabulary, but later access language structures in texts that use the same techniques.

COMPREHENSION STRATEGIES

In our teaching of reading we emphasize comprehension strategies. By doing this the kids become critical readers and thinkers and begin to question what they are hearing and reading, and even writing. In first and second grade we focus primarily on building background knowledge or new schema, questioning, visualizing, inferring, determining importance (How can I use this new knowledge to help me understand? Can I apply it when I need it?), summarizing, and synthesizing. A brief description of these strategies follows:

Questioning	Thoughtful readers ask questions to clarify something they don't understand, to resolve problems, to discover new information, and to understand what they read. "I wonder . . ."
Schema	Thoughtful readers use their schema, or what they know and their prior experiences, to improve their understanding and pleasure of the text.
Make Connections	Thoughtful readers make connections to their lives, to other texts, and to the world. When children are able to make connections, it helps them understand and enjoy what they read.
Sensory Images	Thoughtful readers use their schema and five senses to create mental images to enhance their understanding and enjoyment of the text.
Infer	Thoughtful readers use their schema and information or clues from the text to derive conclusions about the text. "What do you think will happen?"
Determine Importance	Thoughtful readers decide which ideas are the most important in the text. This helps the children determine what parts of the text are significant and which parts are not as they read.
Synthesize	Thoughtful readers are able to summarize a text, understand its primary ideas, generalize, and develop a new idea, perspective, or way of thinking. *(Harvey and Goudvis 2000 and Keene and Zimmerman 1997)*

As part of this process we keep in mind the information literacy standards as a guide to help us.

> *In an information society, ALL people should have the right to information that can enhance their lives. To promote economic independence and quality of existence, people need to be informed and up-to-date. Out of the overabundance of available information, people need to be able to find and use a variety of information to meet a wide range of personal and business needs. (National Forum on Information Literacy 2005)*

These standards promote a more democratic society, where everyone has access to information. According to the American Library Association the standards include three parts: information literacy, independent learning, and social responsibility.

Activating Our Schema Through Connections

Schema is a good launching point when working on comprehension of texts. Each person has different schema because we all have different life experiences. We tell the kids that we are going to construct schema for new topics. We talk about making connections to what we are reading or an image we are looking at. We try to keep our connections relevant to what we are discussing so they can help us better understand what we are reading and keep our brains active while we read.

We see the kids going to a deeper level of sophistication with their questions and with their reading and writing when they have background knowledge and genuine interest in a topic. A lot of schema activating can be done by using connections. For ELLs connections generate endless topics for them to write about because they are often writing their world. When we say this we mean they not only write about their world, but also they capture the essence of the world around them. It is their world they write, read, and interpret. The types of connections we frequently hear from the kids are text-to-life, text-to-text, and text-to-self. We revisit these connections over and over while reading and point out how the connections show us that our students already have schema on any given topic.

Information Literacy Standards

Information Literacy

Standard 1: The student who is information literate accesses information efficiently and effectively.

Standard 2: The student who is information literate evaluates information critically and competently.

Standard 3: The student who is information literate uses information accurately and creatively.

Independent Learning

Standard 4: The student who is an independent learner is information literate and pursues information related to personal interests.

Standard 5: The student who is an independent learner is information literate and appreciates literature and other creative expressions of information.

Standard 6: The student who is an independent learner is information literate and strives for excellence in information seeking and knowledge generation.

Social Responsibility

Standard 7: The student who contributes positively to the learning community and to society is information literate and recognizes the importance of information to a democratic society.

Standard 8: The student who contributes positively to the learning community and to society is information literate and practices ethical behavior in regard to information and information technology.

Standard 9: The student who contributes positively to the learning community and to society is information literate and participates effectively in groups to pursue and generate information. (American Association of School Librarians 1998)

Their connections range in sophistication and often begin with text-to-self because it is most pertinent to them. It may be as simple as "This book reminds me of when I went on a bike ride with my brother." Later, as they become more familiar with what connections are, they begin to relate the ideas from text-to-text such as, "This story about the grandma reminds me of the book we read called *My Family.* It had a story about a grandma, too." We build on these connections to help them understand the varying texts introduced throughout the year. Later we move beyond connections and begin the discussion of how they are part of our inner conversations or our transactions with the text.

Get Help!

We have learned not only that it is okay to ask for help from other teachers, literacy coaches, outside experts, and even kids, but also that asking adds to our teaching. Now that we have accepted that we can't do everything on our own, we are constantly looking for folks to come in and work with us.

One person we collaborate and coteach with frequently is our library media specialist, Nell. Together we give the students more exposure to comprehension strategies and information literacy during our library time. Nell understands our nonstop day and remains positive about coteaching and collaboration. Our planning time is limited but if Nell isn't teaching when we swing by the library, we discuss what we want to do, where we want to go with it, and why. We generate objectives and teaching points and decide who will do what. Material gathering takes time, so we split up the work and meet back during library time. If we don't have time to find Nell, she finds us! She'll often stop by our rooms and nail down what we are going to do. It has been great. It takes extra time and work to get to know one another and work together, but it has been worthwhile. The better we understand one another's styles, the more powerful our coteaching has become.

A SNAPSHOT OF COLLABORATION AND COTEACHING

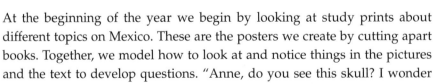

At the beginning of the year we begin by looking at study prints about different topics on Mexico. These are the posters we create by cutting apart books. Together, we model how to look at and notice things in the pictures and the text to develop questions. "Anne, do you see this skull? I wonder why it looks like sugar," Nell says as we look at a study print on the Day of the Dead. "Wow, Nell! I was wondering the same thing!" She takes out a sticky note and writes, "I wonder why the skull looks like sugar" and draws a picture of the skull along with an arrow pointing to the one on the study print. She sticks it right on the print. We continue like this, observing images and writing our "I wonders." This is how we practice questioning.

We are also working on making connections. Kids are always making connections to our studies. We've worked from the first day to make visible what thoughtful readers do. Using their schema and making connections is natural for first and second graders. We want them to make connections between the areas of content study and see that their schema in one area can help them understand something in another area. We have another study print out, but this time it is filled with pictures of cherry trees from Japan. "Anne," Nell says, "I have a connection. The cherry-blossom festival is like the Day of the Dead. It's a celebration."

"You're right, Nell. Hey, what kind of connection is that?"

"Maybe text-to-text, because we read about them in different places?"

"I think you're right!"

"Let's talk about your schema," Nell says as she turns to the class. "Does anyone have a connection?" Thumbs go up.

"I have seen a tree like that near my house," Mario says.

"Great. What kind of connection is that, Mario?" we ask.

"Text-to-life?" His nose crinkles in doubt.

"Exactly!" We write Mario's connection on a sticky note and put it on a piece of chart paper where we are tracking our connections. Nell writes "T-L" for text-to-life so that we will remember. By making these connections we are relating the texts to other areas of our lives to increase comprehension. It also helps us become active with the text as we think about what we are reading. When the kids make connections that seem to diverge from what we are talking about or reading, we accept them as approximations. We can discuss how that connection helps us understand. Often something we think is unrelated actually is providing meaning for the child.

Depending on which comprehension strategy we are working on, Nell builds lessons around it using study prints, fiction and nonfiction texts, or anything she can find that will help the kids understand and practice the strategy. She has been a wonderful asset to our team. Working with the library media specialist this way is refreshing and helps us reinforce what we are doing throughout the day.

Guest Readers and Writers

Our kids love reading to one another—so much so, that the issue of who was going to read to the class at the end of the day became so fraught and competitive that we had to make a sign-up chart to establish some sort of order. (See Figure 4.3.) This chart creates another opportunity for a voluntary literacy event or an opportunity for the kids to read and write because

FIGURE 4.3
The kids sign up to read books to the class.

they really want to. Opportunities like these allow us to authentically assess a child's progress. The kids love reading and sharing so much that they want to share their favorite books, the books they write, and their research. This enthusiasm places them in a time and space where they are able to share what they have learned without feeling nervous or uncomfortable. It's a perfect way for us to observe and listen. As children share, we observe their reading behaviors and note how we can work with them later, either during conferencing or through mini-lessons. We use this time to celebrate their passion for reading.

They read books they have written as well. Mayra sits down in front of the class with her recently published book on the aurora borealis. "'Aurora Borealis,' by Mayra," she says proudly. Mayra has a Big Book that she laboriously researched, wrote, illustrated, and then had us bind with a spiral binding. It's beautiful. It is the root of her newly formed interest in everything Alaska. "I want to go to Alaska when I grow up," she says. She wants to travel everywhere, it seems. Every time she looks at a globe or a map, her mind is flooded with questions. "The aurora borealis is a group of lights in Alaska," she begins. She is so proud of her book that she can't stop smiling. She has everyone's attention.

A PERSONAL REFLECTION

A room full of books, magazines, and comic books sends the message that reading is valued here. We know we are on the right path when we hear adults walking by and asking, "Is this the library?" We have made a huge effort to provide books in home languages for our kids. Because our population is predominantly Latino, we have more books in Spanish, but when we get kids who speak other languages, we do our best to find texts for them. Even if they are in a classroom that is not the "native language" classroom, they still have access to books in different languages. Nell keeps our school library full of great books in Spanish for our Spanish-speaking students.

CHAPTER FIVE

FOSTERING QUESTIONS AND GATHERING INFORMATION

We must strive to create class-rooms that celebrate passionate curiosity. . . . Curiosity spawns questions. Questions clarify confusion. Questions stimulate research efforts. Questions propel us forward and take us deeper into reading. Human beings are driven to find answers and make sense of the world.
(Harvey and Goudvis 2000)

The first step in nonfiction writing is to get students talking about their world and reading and writing their world. The next step is for them to have access to comprehensible texts with fabulous images and to begin reading more of the nonfiction books that interest them. It is then that they begin to formulate questions and we start the more formal process of note taking. All of these things lead to independent inquiry.

HELPING CHILDREN LEARN TO QUESTION

Questioning is the catalyst of inquiry, and we spend a significant amount of time working with the kids to develop it. Lots of first graders still are developing what a question even is, how to ask it, how to use their schema to ask questions, and how to formulate meaningful questions. Spending high-quality time letting the kids explore questioning has been worthwhile because it helps them become more independent in the future.

One approach to begin questioning and developing "I wonders" is to gather images on a specific topic of interest such as natural disasters and use the language frame "I wonder _____? Something exciting! Something adventurous!" The images should be as spectacular and seductive as possible, which means they should be large so the students can see details, should be in color, and should be numerous so that a variety of pictures describe the same topic. They can be straight out of books or magazines, or from on-line resources, calendars, posters, or even postcards. By using a myriad of sources to create collections of images specifically for writing about nonfiction topics, we have introduced more than just books for the kids to think of as nonfiction texts. We use materials such as books, magazines, study prints, clip art, and articles from on-line resources.

Once the pictures have been found, we model how to choose an image that is interesting. We do this through think-alouds. We talk, talk, and talk out loud, saying everything we are thinking. We try to be specific and include even the most mundane thoughts we might be having to make it clear we are grappling with our own ideas. We then place the image on an easel where everyone can see it. We use sticky notes to model the writing to describe the information we see in the image, using writing strategies that have been introduced, reading what is written, and continuing to think aloud. During this time we start asking questions about what we see in the image. (See Figure 5.1.) The questions can range from very simplistic thoughts about the colors, to more complex, abstract thoughts about the purpose of something in a picture or the impact an event has on its surroundings. With images of natural disasters this is easy to do because of their wide range: houses in ruin from earthquakes, volcanoes shooting spectacular lava, tsunamis overtaking cities.

We continue using the phrase "I wonder." (See Figure 5.2.) It is used repeatedly so that the children internalize the vocabulary used to ask a question and so emergent speakers and listeners can begin to access vocabulary. Changing vocabulary can be confusing for ELLs, so initially we don't use several different phrases to describe the same process. For example, we don't say, "I wonder" one moment, then use direct questions such as "Why is lava red?" the next. The purpose of using "I wonder" is that it gives the student ownership of the question and therefore a reason for seeking the answer. As the students become more experienced with asking questions and more familiar with the language structures that are a part of it, we introduce different structures of asking questions without the phrase "I wonder."

GETTING MORE EXPERIENCE WITH NOTE TAKING

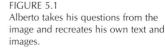

Our next step toward more sophisticated informational writing is to take our knowledge of how to ask and write questions and begin the note-taking process. (See Figure 5.3.) It is important to remember that note taking is the process in which the students read or make observations from a text or image and transfer their thinking onto paper. We say this because note taking can look like a lot of

FIGURE 5.1
Alberto takes his questions from the image and recreates his own text and images.

FIGURE 5.2
A large note-taking poster gives the kids an idea of how to organize their notes.

FIGURE 5.3
Jordan uses arrows to link questions with "found" answers. On-line resources provided Jordan with images to respond to. Jordan reveals her learning of the inside of a pyramid with a cutaway. Students' responses frame the left side of her poster.

different things. It can be writing down questions developed from reading or observing, it can be writing down new information, it can be summarizing a text, and it can even be drawing a pictorial representation of a child's interpretation of a text or picture. This wide range of ways of thinking about note taking helps guide the children as they learn to determine importance and interpret information.

During a mini-lesson for gathering information or taking notes, we begin with posting objectives, to make it clear to everyone what we are focusing on, and to ensure there is a little ambiguity about what we will be doing. During the note-taking lesson the objective might be "We are writing our thinking down as notes." We are putting our writing and our thinking down for all to see, learn from, and respond to. Also posted is a language frame: "I noticed you _____ and I also saw you _____." The kids can use this frame when we ask them to tell us what they saw us doing.

We start simply by holding a large picture of an image of the coral reef and begin to think aloud. "If you listen and watch, you will know what to do, because you're going to do what we do." Step by step we pull out observations about the image and use the language frame "I wonder _____." "I wonder what kinds of fish live in the coral reef." We quickly draw a picture of the fish in the coral reef. Beginning with a two-column note-taking sheet makes the task less daunting. We post the note-taking sheet beneath the objective for everyone to see. Each column of the note-taking sheet is labeled with the language frames we are practicing, such as "I wonder _____." and "I learned _____." As the kids gain more experience, different columns can be added. We have experimented with a column on "Connections," another titled "My Schema," one called "Wow!" for really exciting information, another for "My New Schema," and one for "More Questions" to show that note taking is a ongoing process.

We continue the mini-lesson by pointing to our heads. "Ready?" we ask. The kids are all sitting on the floor close to the easel where we're doing our thinking. They find it difficult not to say anything, and if people were watching, they might think, "Why not let them chime in?" Having the kids listen and notice while we think aloud means they tend to watch more closely and are later able to share with each other, then with the group as a whole. It gives them time to think and formulate how they want to express themselves. It is a short mini-lesson, taking only a few minutes, but that goes a long way.

We sometimes model note taking by consolidating a long caption into notes. For instance, "Hot lava exploding from Hawaii's Kilauea reaches high into the night sky and flows quickly down the mountain to the sea, where the cool water hardens the molten lava to rock" might be written as something like "Lava from Kilauea is hot. When it touches water, it hardens," and then we draw an arrow pointing to the picture. We help the students look for important information and summarize or synthesize it. Our hope is to show them that they can write down their own thinking and not just copy the text. This takes time. It is a skill that will help them throughout the inquiry process and beyond. (See Figures 5.4 and 5.5.)

We aim for all of this modeling within five to ten minutes. Although it may seem like a lot of modeling in a short period of time, remember that this same activity will be repeated throughout the process of gradually releasing students to do nonfiction inquiry. Thus, they will have multiple opportunities

FIGURE 5.4
We scaffold Yok's note taking by helping him read the text and
summarize it.

FIGURE 5.5
Kent and his crocodile friend grin as he studies these ferocious animals.
The book's compelling images provided him with the opportunity to
talk, draw, and write.

to practice. Additionally, the short segments of focused practice simplify the
process and make it more accessible to ELLs. When the kids know that they
are going to be able to do this same activity, their anticipation builds. It is
important to honor this eagerness quickly and let them work instead of
keeping them trapped in group for what to them seems like an eternity.

The kids like to make their thinking big and visible. We can accommodate that easily. Once we've modeled what to do and the kids have shared
their thinking, they are ready to get to work. We use large sheets of heavier
paper and make our same columns on that. The students grab note-taking
sheets and at least four sticky notes, clipboards, and pens, and go to work
independently on texts of their choice. As the kids work, we walk around
the room, conferring with them one-on-one. After about fifteen or twenty
minutes the group reconvenes and the students share their new learning.
The sharing of their thinking is similar to the session in which they talked
about what they saw the teacher doing in terms of language structure and
format. Again we provide a language structure that we post above where
we are working and that the ELL students can follow. For example, "I
learned _____," or "I wonder _____." After the children have shared, we
go back and review all the new information they have learned to synthesize
the activity and bring it full circle. We like to emphasize the amount of information they were able to find about any given topic. It is a good idea to pull
samples from the kids' work to share as examples. This will happen repeatedly, so it gives us the opportunity to share each and every child's work
eventually. Kids comment on what they know about the subject, and sometimes the allure is so strong they want to work together in pairs or small
groups for a while. When this happens, we let them.

Using the giant note taking charts is an extension of the mini-lessons on determining importance from text and of the images on how to take notes. We do all the modeling to show how to write down important words, writing our "I wonders" and showing our thinking with comments and connections. We demonstrate what strategic thinking looks like; they see us doing it and are eager to try it on their own topics. The kids add an image to each piece of text on the note-taking chart. With a highlighter in hand we read the text and talk about what's important, highlighting some of the important words. We are interacting with the text to pull out important or interesting information. The kids see us highlighting, drawing arrows, and underlining words. For instance, Mabel reads the sentence "Insects crawl in the arctic snow and scamper in the desert." We simply highlight part of the sentence and she adds it to her new schema.

Next to "I Learned" and "I Wonder" the kids draw small images of what they have written and color them. Sometimes after the kids have written what they've learned and wondered about and drawn images to represent their words, they have a masterpiece of thinking made visible. They can easily explain what they explored and discovered. (See Figure 5.6.)

What it looks like:

We use a large sheet of paper.

We create two columns ("I Learned," "I Wonder").

We use sticky notes—one color for new learning, one color for questions.

We think aloud and model making mistakes.

We model strategies to get through difficulties.

We write information and questions.

We think aloud where to place each sticky note.

We practice "noticing" what we have done. "What did you see me doing?"

We think-pair-share with a neighbor.

We listen in on kids' conversations.

We ask for responses, then write and post them on the left side.

We gradually release students to do what we did.

Kids can work for fifteen–thirty minutes.

Kids write thinking on sticky notes.

Kids draw small symbolic representations to connect to text.

We regroup and share some of what we learned. Kids place sticky notes on chart.

We put them on posters.

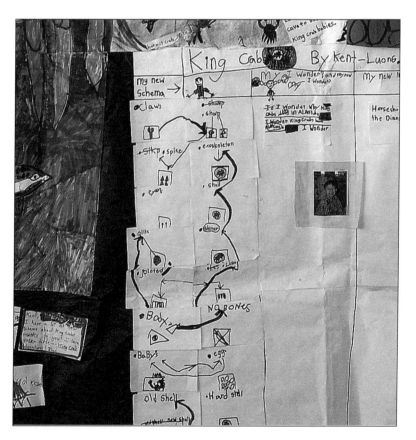

FIGURE 5.6
These king crab notes are carefully organized and categorized with arrows directing the reader.

BENEFITS FOR ELLS

Giant Notes

✓ Giant notes can easily be differentiated, depending on language experience.

✓ Kids can move sticky notes around and get experience organizing information.

✓ Writing notes gives ELLs practice determining what is important and gathering information.

✓ Kids get practice talking about their notes in both whole-group and one-on-one settings.

✓ Information is easily posted and read by others.

A PERSONAL REFLECTION

One question that comes up frequently is, What do we do with a brand new English speaker? The first thing we think of is to use enhanced learning techniques. These techniques increase comprehensible input while reducing a child's affective filter and have been the most successful tools for us while in a whole-group setting, but this isn't enough. By using a gradual-release-of-responsibility framework, we free ourselves up to work with them to do some of the following things once the other kids are working independently.

We can do more intense vocabulary practice using images and orally practicing language structures. For instance, the fishbowl activity is a good one. Kids sit in two concentric circles. The kids in the outside circle ask a question such as, "What is that?" The kids in the inside circle hold up a card with an image of an insect (for example) and answer, "This is a butterfly." The kids in the inside circle stand up and move clockwise until each child has had a chance to practice the language structure.

We use texts with compelling images that connect the picture with simple text. The language structures used for asking questions and answering can be differentiated depending on the sophistication of the child's English language development.

We can reread texts we have seen in whole group, moving through them more slowly, emphasizing important words, using gestures and even realia if necessary.

As their English progresses, we can scribe their thinking.

We can develop mini-lessons around any given topic that will give the kids more practice with the activity we are working on.

The idea is to make sure that whatever they are doing is pertinent to the content or topic the rest of the class is studying. We keep in mind that this is a long journey we are taking together and that patience is a huge part of it.

CHAPTER SIX

GUIDED INQUIRY

One unit we do to help build the independence that the kids need to finally leap into their own inquiries is about insects. We start by finding lots of sets of books with gripping images. We've been able to locate some Big Books as well as multiple sets with text and images that are accessible and have well illustrated images or vibrant photographs. We have also made posters about different insects. We've found information that we could adapt for first graders and printed color images from the Internet, then put the text and images together. They are great because they allow each kid to have his or her own poster to work from.

To kick off the unit we simply begin reading the books we've gathered. Once we start reading, the kids take over with their enthusiasm for the topic. The pictures and images of insect close-ups are so exciting for the kids, they cannot contain themselves. Then there are the real insects.

In a video that was shot in Brad's room, over scenes of kids closely observing a praying mantis, educational consultant Nancy Commins talks about content that "lends itself to be touched, looked at, to be photographed, to be talked about, in a way that is concrete at first but allows for expanded and more abstract thinking in relationship to something that is more visible" (Goudvis and Harvey 2005). We go outside, and without going too far are able to find many species of insects in the grass, trees, and bushes. We find they are everywhere! Soon we have jars of insects in our room, creating an insect museum. Every so often we need to let them go because we have too many. We also have a mantis in our classroom for the kids to observe and to care for, and there is always great concern for how it is doing. This has partly solved the issue of too many insects, because the bees, stingers and all, provide a nutritious and varied diet for our class mantis! Nancy Commins is right: talking about what we are seeing in real life keeps our discussion contextual and authentic.

Together we begin to come up with some "I wonders" and other thinking about our reading. Sometimes we stop as we are reading and think aloud, although quite often the kids are making their inner conversations audible. They just start wondering and thinking aloud. We encourage this, because one child's question often leads to other kids thinking more about the topic. With sticky notes handy, we write the questions down to keep a record of our thinking. We put these notes on a giant note-taking sheet. We organize them and sort them according to topics. The kids have already drawn little images on the notes, which makes it easy to classify them. We go through this process for the different columns on our note-taking sheet. This gives us lots of practice before the kids begin to work on their own. We are viewing texts, writing, drawing images, and talking about what we see, read, and write. At each phase we stop and have conversations about where their thinking comes from and why they want to know more. This helps our community learn from each other and also helps the kids develop more pertinent questions. We want to clarify that by using columns we are not trying to limit the kids' thinking to a linear way of learning; rather we use them as a scaffold to help them organize it. They build schema, which leads them into formulating more sophisticated questions and connecting their thinking and learning, rather than just spouting off what they know or what they wonder. It allows them to look at learning as an ongoing process rather than something that starts and finishes.

Another fun way to model is to create our own inquiries and go through the steps with the kids. As each inquiry is constructed, we can explicitly model each aspect such as strategic reading, developing questions, note taking, synthesizing, illustrating, and using nonfiction features (labeling, using captions, adding a title). This can be done slowly. The kids become interested in the project and start to help by looking for books, bringing images to share, and using on-line resources. It helps create the disposition of being part of a community of thinkers.

INTEGRATE NEW VOCABULARY WHILE DOING INQUIRIES

The insect books, magazines, and posters provide us with lots of great new words. Keeping in mind that we want to keep our thinking visible, we have a discussion about making a word wall with only insect words. (See Figure 6.1.) That way we can look up and learn the meaning of new, interesting words and even spell them like scientists do. As we read, the kids tell us to write some new vocabulary, and we add it to the list with other words. For

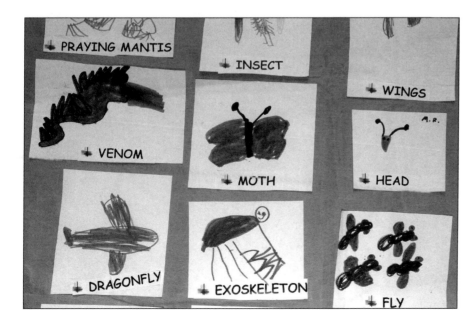

FIGURE 6.1
Kid-generated word walls give the kids more access to meaningful print.

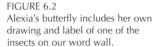

FIGURE 6.2
Alexia's butterfly includes her own drawing and label of one of the insects on our word wall.

example, words such as *segment, exoskeleton, legs,* and *antennae* are a few that we come up with. Now we type the new vocabulary words in a large bold font so they will be readable, and later the kids will write and draw their own. The word wall goes up for all to see and use and surrounds us with the content we are studying. It is an opportunity to differentiate text as well. Some images may have single word labels, such as "dragonfly," whereas others may use a more complex structure such as "Dragonflies have four wings and antennae." (See Figure 6.2.)

Finally the time comes for each child to choose what he wants to study. At this point the kids have been exposed to a variety of texts on different insects through the guided practice, and most of them have an idea of what they want to study. Rarely are kids at the same place with what they are studying, and therefore they tend to start in different places. Some of them get going immediately, whereas others still need assistance in looking for information that sparks their interest. We are there to help. (See Figure 6.3.)

Kent is starting out by illustrating his dragonfly research with the help of a pile of insect books in front of him. Tristian is using sticky notes to write what she is learning and wondering about. Yok and David are on the computer checking out insects from an on-line museum and having a conversation about what they notice. David will continue exploring and

FIGURE 6.3
Cricket's songs fill our ears.

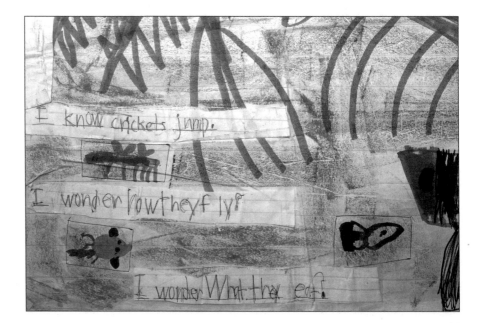

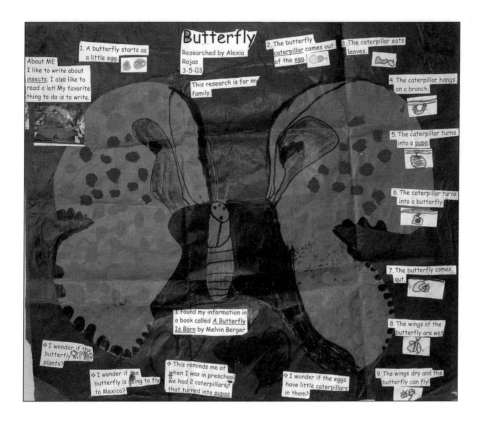

Butterfly
Researched by Alexia Rojas
3-5-03

About ME
I like to write about insects. I also like to read a lot! My favorite thing to do is to write.

This research is for my family.

1. A butterfly starts as a little egg.

2. The butterfly caterpillar comes out of the egg.

3. The caterpillar eats leaves.

4. The caterpillar hangs on a branch.

5. The caterpillar turns into a pupa.

6. The caterpillar turns into a butterfly.

7. The butterfly comes out.

8. The wings of the butterfly are wet.

I found my information in a book called *A Butterfly Is Born* by Melvin Berger

9. The wings dry and the butterfly can fly!

❖ I wonder if the butterfly will eat plants?

❖ I wonder if the butterfly is going to fly to Mexico?

❖ This reminds me of when I was in preschool we had 2 caterpillars that turned into pupas.

❖ I wonder if the eggs have little caterpillars in them?

FIGURE 6.4
Alexia, working in her L2, took her thinking about butterflies public. She painted first then added her text, which we typed up.

eventually create large beetle posters with his thinking on the subject. Alexia will paint a giant butterfly with fluorescent paint. (See Figure 6.4.) Yok will make a huge bee and write a few sentences to add to his information. (See Figure 6.5 and color insert 2.) This is all natural. The kids are everywhere, spread out with their work, engaged in their thinking, working at their own pace. We move around the room conferring with kids, helping them move from one step to the next. Some of them might start by taking notes, and others start with their illustrations and art—it's all good. It is a cyclical process, and each of them will work in his or her own way. Inquiry projects can last anywhere from a few days to several weeks, depending on their complexity and on how much time each day is dedicated to inquiry.

We note approximations during these times of independent inquiry. After conferring with Alexia we write down what we noticed in her thinking. We notice her strengths, and what she is attempting or approximating in her exploration of her topic, and we notice her use of her interlanguage, or second language. With ELLs we are conscious of their approximations in English and the implications they have for us as teachers. We observe how the kids use their new language and if there are things we can do to help them along the way. Contextual teaching is our focus. However, we also make explicit the nuances of the language. We want them to know

Some Scaffolding Strategies for Inquiry Projects
Drawing first
Lines for words
Invented spelling
Scribing
Word wall
Compelling images
Guided practice
Modeling
Post essential questions
Post objectives
Preview/review
Use of sticky notes
Graphic organizers
Variety of texts
Language frames

Honey Bee

Honey s loopheiter,
On its legs it harbasket.

I know crickets can eat.

FIGURE 6.5
Yok uses art to make meaning with
his bee research.

that people are going to expect them to use standard English, so we show them what that looks like as they are working toward publishing their information. As an example, we can look at verb endings, cognates (words that are related in spelling and meaning in two languages, such as *instrucción* and *instruction*), and the use of articles and give a quick mini-lesson. This is another strategy we have to help the kids develop their comprehension of their new language.

As they work, we set up a matrix for them to distribute, organize, share, and notice commonalities among their thinking. This might have categories such as insects with wings, insects with six legs, special parts, what they eat, and anything else the kids come up with. They add to this matrix as they work on their inquiries and as interesting and important information that they think is relevant comes up. They often use and refer to it for many different reasons such as developing further questions, answering a question they have, getting ideas for future inquiries, and vocabulary building. It synthesizes the entire community's thinking.

STAGES OF INQUIRY AND PUBLISHING

As we have worked on using nonfiction as a tool in literacy development with our ELLs, we have been creating a framework that helps us put all of their work in perspective and gives us a way to look at it and help them become more sophisticated researchers. It can be used as an assessment tool, yet we look at it as a framework to help guide us in how to differentiate. It includes different attributes that we look for, but we want to make clear that they can be recursive and nonlinear. For example, a child may be independent in her work on design and illustration of an inquiry, yet emergent in formulating questions and writing down her thinking. The kids can move back and forth through these stages. We use the information by noticing the kids' approximations in their inquiries. This is not meant to be a rubric, which we see as limiting and something that can turn into a checklist, but rather as a guide to help us see where the kids are and as a way to further develop a common language to communicate with one another. This helps us work with them to move to the next phase. With advanced attributes we see more independence. However, it is still important to model, confer,

Emergent Researcher	Intermediate Researcher	Advanced Researcher
Uses images to gather information and ask questions with teacher support.	Uses images to gather information and ask questions with decreasing teacher support. Begins to use text to gather information.	Uses images and text to gather information and ask questions with little support.
Note taking done by teacher as a scribe.	Note taking done with decreased teacher scribing and more use of framed sentences. Increased use of standard English structure and grammar.	Writes independently with a variety of language structures. Uses standard English structure and grammar more consistently.
Develops questions with teacher support.	Develops questions with decreasing teacher support and more use of framed questions.	Develops questions independently and uses new schema to develop new questions.
Notices/observes nonfiction text features and gathers information from them with teacher support.	Begins to notice/observe nonfiction text features and uses them to learn/wonder more, with decreasing teacher support. Begins to incorporate the features in own research.	Independently uses text features to further develop schema and questions. Uses them in own inquiries.
Searches for possible answers to questions with teacher support.	Searches for possible answers to questions and starts to look for important information within the text with decreasing teacher support.	Searches for possible answers to questions and determines importance of text independently.
Finds and uses a variety of nonfiction sources and materials with teacher support.	Finds and uses a variety of nonfiction sources and materials with decreasing teacher support.	Finds and uses a variety of nonfiction sources and materials independently.
Organizes information and thinking on poster with teacher support. Questions and new schema may or may not be related to one another.	Organizes information and thinking on poster with decreasing teacher support. Begins to make connections between questions and new schema.	Organizes information and thinking on poster independently. Can make connections between questions and new schema alone.
Completes other attributes of inquiry poster: title, researcher, illustrator, dedication, "about me," "what I did," "write your questions and comments here," "add your schema," "where I found my information," with teacher support.	Completes other attributes of inquiry poster: title, researcher, illustrator, dedication, "about me," "what I did," "write your questions and comments here," "add your schema," "where I found my information," with decreasing teacher support.	Completes other attributes of inquiry poster: title, researcher, illustrator, dedication, "about me," "what I did," "write your questions and comments here," "add your schema," "where I found my information," independently.
Creates illustrations or uses photos, color copies, magazine cutouts to help express information.	Creates illustrations that increase in detail and sophistication to document thinking. Begins to create relationships between text on poster and images.	Creates detailed and sophisticated illustrations that are directly related to the text she has written on her poster.
Presents information with teacher support.	Presents information with decreasing teacher support.	Presents information Independently.
Beginning to synthesize thinking by having conversations with teacher.	Synthesis of thinking becoming more sophisticated. Teacher continues to support and prompt.	Can synthesize thinking independently and does so with little prompting from the teacher.

teach, and guide them to their next step. For example, Cesar is an emergent researcher and is using images primarily to gather information and develop questions. As a next step we would look for materials that slowly introduce text with labels or short captions and are accessible to him so that he begins to practice looking for information not only within the images, but also within the text.

SYNTHESIZING OUR THINKING

After about a month of reading, exploring, writing, and publishing our insect thinking, we begin to wrap up the unit. A great way to do a synthesis of all the things we know is to make a mind map. We act as the scribe and guide the kids' thinking: "Let's make something really cool that shows all of what we learned and know about insects." We have a large sheet of white paper taped up against an easel. Some thick black markers are within reach. We've also cut up little squares for illustrating. We activate their schema by making a connection to their learning. "Remember the mind maps we made when we studied families, plants, Mexico, Japan, earthquakes, and tsunamis? Now we are going to make one for insects."

Mind maps were developed in the late 1960s by Tony Buzan and use a range of skills such as word, image, number, logic, rhythm, color, and spatial awareness. Buzan's own words about how he conceived mind maps pinpoint what we constantly see happen to ELLs. They are boxed into one way of doing things and can't explore other ways of expression. He once said,

> Again like all children, I was both excited and afraid at the prospect of learning to write: it seemed such a mystical and magical skill. At first I loved it, drawing big letters in many colors on large sheets of paper, but gradually became less enchanted, when I had to make my writing smaller and smaller (I wanted to do Big curves and tall lines, and my teachers wanted everything small, and compact in order to "be neat" and to save paper). In addition my freedom was beginning to be restricted as I was increasingly obliged to write on lines, and not to go under or over them at the "wrong" times. (Buzan 2005)

Why constrict them? Why not help them share their thinking and make it big? For us, the thought of being neat translates into stifling creativity and inhibits our ELLs' ability to communicate with us in various forms.

Our mind map starts in the middle and fans out with stems like a giant colorful flower. Each stem has a specific meaning, which the kids construct with us. With the vocabulary in plain site, we ask, "What should the main idea for our mind map be?" We point to the paper with a circle drawn in the middle as we talk about it. "Insects!" seems to be the unanimous thought. We write it like that—"Insects!" with an exclamation mark. "What should we draw to represent insects?" We point to the word and pictures of insects posted on the word wall or matrix of special parts. Of course everyone has an idea of an insect to draw, from mantises to bees, moths, and butterflies. "Let's come back to that. Add it to your mental list so you'll remember what you want to draw for a symbolic representation of insects." Again, we refer to the word and picture on the word wall. The kids are familiar with this vocabulary because we have been using it in context and have been expecting them to use it, and they do.

The main idea or center of the mind map remains blank except for the word *insects.* Later we will come back to it to add images to represent this main idea. We do this to create a little bit of momentum and move on to making the first stem of our mind map. We want to get a little jump, but not too big of one. "Let's make a stem and we'll go back to the central theme." It is important to keep referring to the word wall or matrix so the kids can make connections between the text and images. Taking the marker, we draw a curving stem, or branch. "Let's think a minute. What information should we put on this stem?" It is quiet, except for some small whispers. We have a finger pointing to our head and one on our lips. After a minute, we say, "Tell someone next to you what you think we should put on our first stem." We are also pointing, using gestures, and speaking slowly and as clearly as possible. We come up with insects that fly and ones that don't. We start listing insects that fly on one side; later we will add the nonflying insects on the other. With a mind map, comparing and contrasting is easy to do. And because every piece of text has a symbolic representation attached to it, the intended thinking is clear. (See Figure 6.6.)

Bees, beetles, moths, mantises, and butterflies begin our list of flying insects. We write them down, being sure to leave space so our words are easy to read. With some small squares of white construction paper we model making an insect to represent bees. Pulling out a book nearby, we open it and find an image of one. We just draw what we see, taking our time to add colors and make it vibrant, talking as we do it. Then we say, "Do we want to make a little pop-up? Yeah, that would be

FIGURE 6.6
As a group the kids distribute their thinking by creating an insect mind map.

fun!" We cut our little bee and use a piece of scrap paper to make a mini-accordion, glue it on the back of the bee, and think out loud: "Let's see, we want to put this by the word bees." We glue it on the map, next to the word. Well aware that the kids are champing at the bit, we tell them, "Think for a minute." We point to our watch and point again to our head. "Think what you noticed us doing. Now tell someone next to you what we did." Feeling confident that they know what to do, we let them pick which insect they would like to represent. This time we work in front of our new mind map on the floor. We have images of insects posted; we have our insect word wall, our matrix, their research, and books and magazines at hand. We hand out the little squares of paper, asking the kids what they want to do. Scissors, markers, and scraps of construction paper are all within reach. The kids excitedly get to work drawing.

After a bit of time we stop and say, "Let's come together and share." It takes some time for everyone to switch gears, and some kids are finishing up. "Who made a bee?" A couple of thumbs pop up, and we look at the kids, who then come up and glue their insects on the map. The kids glue their symbolic representation next to the text, which we have already written. We proceed in this manner, adding and representing little bits of information one at a time. If we sense they are tired or not really enthusiastic at the moment, we don't force it, because we want to make it interesting, worthwhile, and fun. And because we eventually want the kids to be able to make their own mind maps, we want to make it a positive experience. We take our time with our mind map and let it extend throughout a week or longer. The mind map stays up with a "Thinking in Progress" label, because kids naturally want to add to it and talk about it, also holding true to our belief about the power of peripheral stimuli, or learning from our surroundings.

As the week continues, we make a stem for legs, special parts, and insect bodies. As we make our group insect mind map, we are talking about how to make it more readable by spreading out the stems and text for easier reading, and connecting every piece of information with an image or symbolic representation. We can add anything we want as long as we can explain it. We finish by presenting it to each other. We model how to present, then let the kids take turns doing the stems. We happily observe the kids connecting all the information that surrounds them when presenting the mind map. As they present, connections pop up, and they step over and point to a word on the word wall or to a poster. They do this without any explicit modeling on our part. When we are finished, they are well on their way to creating their own maps—and look how much we have learned about insects!

We finish this unit with a lot of energy, and the kids immediately want to start another inquiry. At this point we work with them to find something that interests them and they begin to explore different topics. This is really exciting to watch, because it shows us how motivated they are to keep learning and wondering about their world.

A PERSONAL REFLECTION

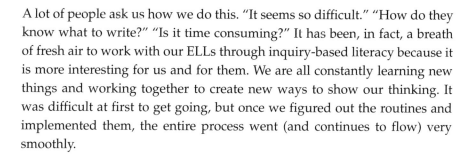

A lot of people ask us how we do this. "It seems so difficult." "How do they know what to write?" "Is it time consuming?" It has been, in fact, a breath of fresh air to work with our ELLs through inquiry-based literacy because it is more interesting for us and for them. We are all constantly learning new things and working together to create new ways to show our thinking. It was difficult at first to get going, but once we figured out the routines and implemented them, the entire process went (and continues to flow) very smoothly.

CHAPTER SEVEN

MOVING INTO INDEPENDENT INQUIRY–KEEP THE QUESTIONS COMING!

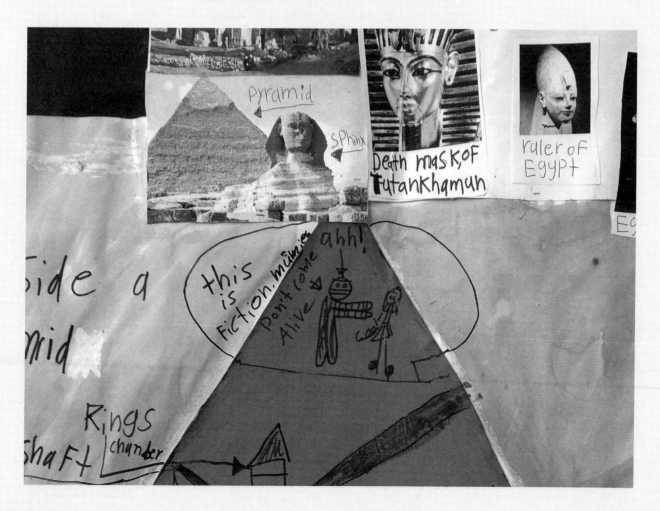

The important thing is to not stop questioning.—Einstein

We finish a mini-lesson on writing what we notice from images, and the kids are released one by one to either work on their research in progress or begin something new. After all the kids are busy, we get up and begin moving from child to child. Some children work alone, and others are in small groups.

Pedro is working near the door with his shark research poster spread out. He is surrounded by markers, sticky notes, and cups of paint. He is busy painting a shark and has written, "I learned most sharks have five gills" on a green sticky note.

Jordan is on the other side of the room just beginning research on sea horses. She has three books that she got from the library. Her clipboard is within reach, and on it she has placed red, yellow, and green sticky notes and a pen. Sitting on the floor next to her is Cloe, who is starting to piece together her research, which she has divided between rays and dolphins. She has paint, glue, her clipboard, and her books beside her, too. Outside the classroom door some kids are spread out on the cafeteria floor with research posters in progress about whale sharks and other sea creatures. Some of these projects are coming close to the size of a whale shark, which is why we had to find somewhere to spread out. These big projects started out very small, usually with one "I learned" or "I wonder."

Gradually the kids gather more "wonders" and more information, and draw and write about them. Stepping back inside the room, Mayra and Denise are working in our little classroom library. Mayra is painting sea otters while Denise is writing on a sentence strip—just a strip of paper—about what she learned about beluga whales. We are moving from one student to another. That's how we often do it. We also use this time to work with a small group who might need similar assistance. With Javier, Yuli, and Alexis, we regroup and work together to get started on a project. This means finding something they are interested in. Javier is interested in thresher sharks and later giant squids, while Alexis and Yuli browse through books looking for something they are curious about.

LETTING THINKING AND LEARNING HAPPEN THROUGH CHOICE

I love to do research because I love to read and use my brain.—Yok

By listening to their conversations and stories we learn from the children what their interests are and what matters to them. "Students should choose the greater proportion of their writing topics," Donald Graves (1985) tells us, but he also notes that their choosing shouldn't exist in a vacuum. Listening to them helps us guide them into their work and show them where to find information, and puts them in control of what they write about or which kind of nonfiction inquiry they choose to do. We let them

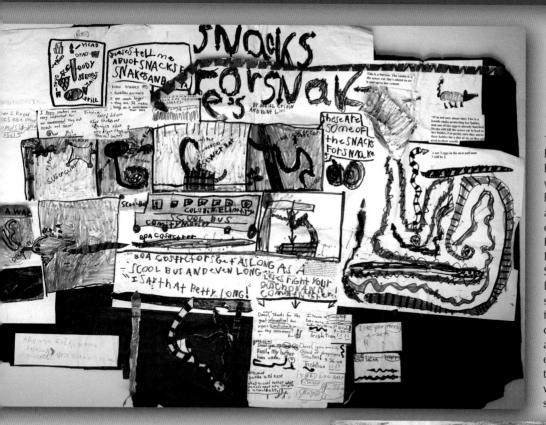

1. Snacks for Snakes began as a solo project by Daniel until Kent walked by, sat down and began talking to Daniel about snakes. This conversation prompted Kent to collaborate with Daniel. Snacks for Snakes demonstrated Daniel and Kent's synthesis of nonfiction features. They included cut-aways, comparisons, a key, labels, and captions with the addition of "Please tell me what you know about snacks for snakes."

2. Yok wanted to take his thinking about honeybees public. Our school library provided him with a stack of books about bees and insects. Together we read and talked about bees. Yok was emerging as a reader and writer, so we scribed some of our insect conversation on sticky notes. Yok wrote his words on white sentence strips and glued them on to his poster. He then drew a large honeybee flying in search of flowers.

3. (top) A conversation with a friend about pandas launched Yuli into her inquiry. We observed Yuli moving naturally back and forth between drawing, writing, reading, and talking about pandas.

4. (bottom) Lupita used her biliteracy in Spanish and English to create "A Mexico Celebration." Lupita's Mexico word wall in Spanish, her heritage language, framed her narrative in her L2, or second language. Her art made people passing by her poster stop, look, read, think, and talk. With "Mexico Celebration," Lupita celebrated her biliterate identity.

Mexico Celebration
By : Lupita Martinez
I ate tamales and drank chocolate at our party. We drew. My big sisters came. In Anne's class we read a book about the Aztecs. In Brad's class we read our Mexico books.

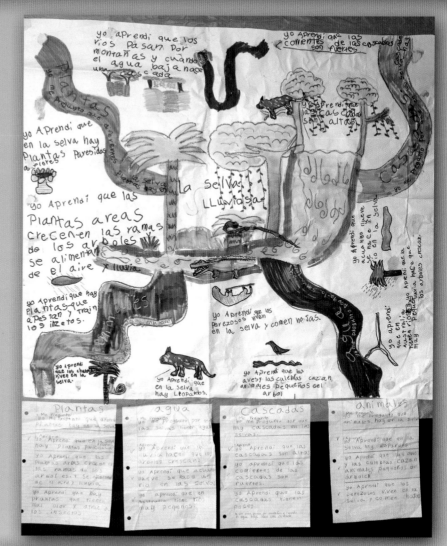

5. Brayan had spent several weeks working with Nell, our media specialist, on his rain forest research. He did a lot of reading in English and Spanish and then decided to make a mind map in Spanish (his L1, or heritage language) to share everything he had learned. He spent a significant amount of time planning out what each stem would represent and how he was going to paint and draw the images that would go with them. The centerpiece, which tells us that his research is about the rain forest, overflows with colors and cascading waterfalls. Each bit of information is accompanied by pop-up animals or exotic drawings of information he gathered and analyzed. He was so excited, that when he finished, Nell was the first person he wanted to share with—and in English, his L2!

6. Kent worked on his "King Crab Adventures" for two months. We left his poster hanging and visible in the classroom until he thought he was finished. Kent taught us that the longer the kids have to work, the more complex their projects will be. His art captured everyone's attention. Kent used arrows in his notes to categorize similar information about king crabs.

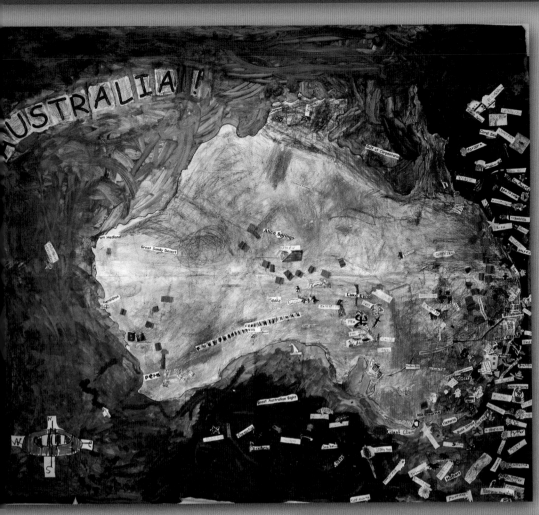

7. We launched our unit on Australia by creating a giant map with paint and oil pastels. Pop-up cities, mountain ranges, sea life, and other features the kids found important or interesting were gradually added, often as voluntary literacy events. The kids wrote small labels for each piece added. This giant map hung in our room for two months and created momentum for our content unit.

8. August loved to make his letters very large and colorful. He taught us that the text can be art alone. August, like Monet, went on to use his colored markers as an impressionist and draw Uluru in Australia.

choose topics, whether it is with their personal narratives or with inquiries, because choice energizes them.

> Choice generates curiosity and adventurous thinking.
> Choice creates momentum.
> Choice allows for more in-depth inquiry.
> Choice encourages independence and builds self-esteem.
> Choice makes learning matter to the kids.
> Choice encourages metacognition and reflection.

By giving them the opportunity to choose we are giving them the opportunity to think and to explore what is relevant and pertinent to them. This drives their learning, and rarely do we find that kids are distracted or bored when they are working on something that they've chosen.

With their choices exploding in their brains kids burst into their explorations with nonfiction. As Yok said while reading some insect books and taking notes, "My brain is so full of images that it's going to explode into tiny popcorn pieces!" As they internalize the thinking routines, we sometimes forget all the time we took to get to this point of independence. The kids enjoy sharing what they know and have done with others in their learning community.

Sometimes kids have a topic in mind and just have to express it on paper and make it visible. Often this happens quickly when they have free time to read or write. Alexia has paper, scissors, and a stapler. Up goes some paper: a sea turtle is put together with two pieces of paper stapled and stuffed together so the shell is puffed out. Legs and head are attached. Lots of background knowledge is at work here. Sometimes kids will approach each other and lend what they know, whether it be information or ideas for art. Soon there are two more girls working, so now three girls are working together. The other girls finish helping Alexia make her sea turtle creations and move on to read. None of this was planned. All it took was time to let them explore and be spontaneous.

Now we come by and ask what she is doing. Alexia explains that she is making a poster about sea turtles. She begins talking about what she knows. Quickly grabbing a pen and some sticky notes, we scribe what she says. "Sea turtles are reptiles," she says. We write it down on a sticky note and place it on her paper. She quickly writes on a sentence strip what she said and begins talking more about sea turtles. "They live in the ocean." Sometimes Alexia uses some approximations in her English syntax, and we write it in conventional structures so she can see, read, hear, and write it. For example, Alexia says, "Sea turtle can swim far." We write, "Sea turtles can swim far." She had missed the morpheme "s," so we point out to her that she is talking about more than one sea turtle and therefore needs to add an

I got some information from Daniel's research poster but he says that the dragons live in Australia and I don't think so. I am going to look in the book again.—Mario

s to the end of *turtle.* We know to keep listening for similar usage so we can work with her until she internalizes this rule in English.

Luckily we have a little reptile book handy, from one of our book tubs. We flip to the back to the index and find pages and pages on turtles. The book is accessible because it has images with contextual text. Now we read a little bit and find that sea turtles' diet consists of jellyfish, crabs, and sea urchins. New information for us. Together we talk about how we could say that, and come up with "Sea turtles eat jellyfish, crabs, and sea urchins to stay healthy." In this process we are using somewhat of a language frame (Sea turtles eat _____.) that she is comfortable with while adding a little more complexity to the grammatical structure as we write more. As Alexia writes her information, we talk about how we could add a little frame for her to put her image in. This sounds like it takes a long time, but it doesn't. Suddenly from a blank sheet of paper Alexia has three sea turtles popping up and swimming across it and text with what she knows and has learned. As she is working, Alexia will write her "wonders," too. This inquiry is about her today, and tomorrow someone else will be inspired by what she has done.

It's important to note that the kids are deciding for themselves what to explore. We might provide ideas and background knowledge, but they choose. It is also their questions and learning that drive their inquiries. Our goal is for them to follow their wonderings and learning, not ours.

Once the kids begin moving into inquiry projects, they are unstoppable. These inquiries range from animals, the ocean, continents, countries, and people, to plants, insects, UFOs, and the solar system. Not only are the students free to choose their topics, but they begin to critically analyze their world, too. The kids might come to learn that pandas are endangered animals and continue to explore the cause of that, or find out that the dead bodies of the orca pods off the coast of Washington are classified as a toxic waste site. This learning often leads to more questions and might lead to action through letter writing or creating a poster showing their new learning and wonderings. They do as many inquiries as they like throughout the year.

CONTINUE BUILDING SCHEMA

The entire time we are working on inquiry, we are simultaneously developing new schema, something we explicitly point out to the kids. We continue to add to our schema anchor charts, we track our schema by writing it down on sticky notes and charting it, and we have discussions about how our schema helps us understand what we read and how it can help us develop new questions. We use the kids' quotes as examples when working on the anchor charts. For example, with a poster we made about schema we took quotes from the kids' conversations about reading and writing and put them together, then used them as a teaching tool to show what schema is. "Tigers have orange and black stripes," Brandon said. "Cheetahs are the ones with spots." We use this quote to point out that he is sharing his schema. Getting them to be conscious of the fact that they know a lot is fun. Once they realize they are experts, they take off running.

Because the kids have a variety of reading levels and differing amounts of schema about chosen topics, we lend more of a hand in certain situations than in others. As we described earlier, we do a lot of modeling at the beginning. This helps us assess where the kids are, and allows them to practice and visualize what is going on. Every step of the way we work with them either through conferring or mini-lessons to ensure they are on the path they want to be, to help them move along at a reasonable pace, and to assess them on the go to drive instruction.

Yuliana at first appears very shy. For a long time she would not say anything, but we noticed her talking and laughing with her friends when they were reading and writing. When we kneel down beside her on the floor, she has a book about endangered animals open to a page on giant pandas. "What are you reading about?" we ask.

"Pandas," Yuli replies.

"Would you like to research about pandas? Other kids would love to learn about them, and you could teach them. What do you think?"

"Okay. I want to do it," she responds. Yuliana is surrounded by other kids' research posters on topics ranging from rabbits to volcanoes. For these first graders animals seem a common and natural choice. While learning about the many animals we also explore political and physical geography. We will come to learn that pandas live in the mountains of China. Yuli knows what to do next. Although she has just moved back from Arizona after being there for six months, she hasn't forgotten our routines. She grabs some pink sticky notes and writes, "I learned." On yellow sticky notes she writes, "I wonder," and on green sticky notes she writes "Wow!" Yuli uses our note-taking anchor chart to guide her in how she can use different-colored sticky notes to help organize her information.

We use the encyclopedia-type book she has open to the information on giant pandas. We look at the pictures and read the text, noticing that giant armadillos and giant otters fill the nearby pages. The text is too difficult for Yuli, so we read it aloud, stopping and rereading parts that are attention grabbing. "Should we write some thinking on the sticky notes?" we ask. Yuli looks up and says, "Pandas are black and white."

We model for her how to write what she said on another sticky note so she can see what it looks like. Below her words she draws a small representation of her text. This image will help her later when she makes large illustrations for her research.

She uses the note-taking anchor chart with the words "I learned," "I wonder," and "Wow" posted at eye level for the kids to use as support. As a class we've used this chart for many mini-lessons on researching and reading nonfiction texts. The large chart serves as a bridge to independence because the kids can use it as a resource for spelling and remembering the sequence of getting their thinking down on different-colored sticky notes. So Yuli is able to begin writing her words that are written down next to her. After she writes her first "I learned," we ask her, "What do you want to do next? Maybe we should reread it."

"Let's read it again," she says. This time we stop reading at where we find that giant pandas eat bamboo.

"What do you think, Yuli—do you want to tell other kids what pandas eat?" we ask. Yuli says, "I learned it eats bamboo."

This time she picks up her pen and begins writing. We point to the word *bamboo* and underline it in pen so she can see how to spell it. With our classroom library books we model for the kids how we can interact with words by using a pen or a highlighter. They see how and why to do it in a real-life way. Now she has written, "I learne it eats bamboo."

She left the *d* off *learned* and we quickly talk about the *ed* ending and tell her to reread her writing since she used *learned* a lot. She then draws a small image of a panda eating bamboo on her sticky note. Yuli has the momentum now to keep writing as we leave to work with some other kids. (See color insert 3.)

While sitting down and talking with Yuli about what she is interested in, we see her change. There is no one to perform for, just a conversation between some classmates and the teacher. Later, after Yuli has filled a few sticky notes with panda schema, we ask, "Yuli, how would you like to show your panda thinking to the class? Would you like to make a book, a poster, or something else?" She has already decided. "A poster!" she says with zeal. Yuli goes over to the computer and reaches below the table for a large square of thick white paper. This works as her starting point for her giant panda research, which will soon turn into five squares glued together side by side. Yuli uses them to write about and draw pandas in different settings, from eating bamboo in the wild to living in the zoo.

SUPPORTING BILINGUALISM AND BILITERACY

We have been experimenting with how and when to support the kids in being bilingual and biliterate. Many schools of thought have pushed us to believe that separation of language is essential when a child is learning to speak a new language. Although we recognize that there are times when this is appropriate, we have discovered that the writing of work in two languages has given us a new perspective into the nature of our students' identities as bilinguals. We share several examples of this here. (See color insert 4.)

FIGURE 7.1
Alexia's work on starfish reflects the development of her biliterate and bilingual identity.

Alexia's Starfish

Alexia has started an inquiry project on starfish while in Spanish literacy. She is so excited about it that she hauls it back to her class where the rest of the day is spent using English. She eagerly asks Brad if she can continue working on her starfish poster. Unbeknownst to us, Alexia begins working in English, and when she is ready, she asks Brad to help her type her words on the computer. Then she shares. She hangs her poster up in the meeting area and calls everyone over. As she begins, she shares in English, reading the Spanish text, translating it in her head, and then saying the words in English. Her poster is filled with information in the two languages and she is able to share it with her audience. It is a classic example of giving the kids the room to be who they are in both languages. (See Figure 7.1.)

Joan and His Hammerhead Sharks

Joan is six years old and reading and writing in both English and Spanish. He is in literacy with Anne and then goes with Brad for an hour of ESL instruction every day. One morning he walks into Brad's room and notices the other kids working on their inquiry projects. "Brad, I want to study sharks, too!" he says.

"Here you go, Joan," Brad says. "Look at these books, and when you're ready, we can sit together to write some of your wonderings." Joan sits on the carpet and browses through the books, placing sticky notes on the pages where he finds interesting information. When he is ready, he and Brad sit down and formulate sentences to articulate his questions and some of the information he has gathered. He has decided he wants to focus on hammerhead sharks. He begins by writing on the sticky notes and then takes a medium-sized piece of white paper and sketches a hammerhead.

The next morning while in literacy with Anne he says, "Can I show you something, Anne?" He takes her hand and leads her into Brad's room. "*Estoy investigando tiburones martillos.*" [I'm doing research on hammerhead sharks.] Joan shows Anne everything he's done so far and then asks if we have any books in Spanish.

"Jaime is working on something about sharks," Anne says. "Let's see if he can share some of his books with you." They go back to Anne's room and sit down with Jaime.

"Jaime, is there anything about hammerhead sharks in those books?" Joan asks.

"What is a hammerhead shark?" Jaime asks.

"Let me see. I'll show you." The two boys begin looking through the books and find several pages dedicated to hammerheads. Joan grabs a pen and begins to jot down information he finds interesting that he hadn't found in the books in English. After about a half hour he gets another sheet of white paper and begins to write this information down and includes drawings to accompany them. He is writing in Spanish.

"Joan, what are you going to do with that information?" Anne asks.

"It's for my hammerhead research," he says. For Joan there is no separation between what he started with Brad in English and what he is continuing to do in Spanish. Over the next couple of weeks Joan adds more and more information to his research. When he is with Brad, he works in English, and when he is with Anne, he works in Spanish. He writes a poem about hammerheads, draws and labels pictures, and ultimately presents his research in both English and Spanish to both classes. Throughout this process we encourage Joan and tell him how cool we think it is that he is working in two languages. His response: "It's because I speak them both." For him the two languages are part of who he is, and his work reflects this. (See Figure 7.2.)

FIGURE 7.2
Joan expresses his dismay about hammerheads being killed.

Celia's Coral Reef

Celia is shy and for a while wouldn't even talk in her first language, Spanish, because of her extreme timidity. She has slowly come out of her shell and now is not afraid to take risks expressing herself in both English and Spanish. Once Celia sees Joan working on his hammerhead project with Brad, she, too, wants to work on an inquiry in English. This transition from Spanish to English is natural for our students, because we have taken the time to coordinate with each other. We try to use common language in terms of the same vocabulary to describe the inquiry process and routines and develop a culture of thinking that supports their curiosity. They don't hesitate to jump into inquiry projects in English, because it is not unknown territory. They have spent time with Anne developing strategies for inquiry that they now apply just in English. Celia begins by dedicating her research to her older sister Mariana, who also was in our class the previous two years. Celia can't wait to show it to her sister, who has been sharing her own writing with Celia for years. Whereas Joan did almost all of his reading and note taking up front, Celia takes a slightly different approach. With each new piece of information she gathers, she wants to add it to her poster. She reads a little bit and finds something exciting, then sits down with bits of paper and illustrates what she has learned, or what she wonders. She works painstakingly like this a little bit each day. While she is with Brad, he sits and works with her, reading with her and helping her take notes, sometimes scribing for her and other times helping her as she writes her words on her own. In Spanish she is a little more independent, and Anne lets her work alone.

"Anne, did you know baby sea horses are only as big as my eyelash?" she comments as she meticulously draws a sea horse, looking at the picture as she goes.

"No! That is so cool!"

"There are jellyfish the size of pennies! That's so small," she says later as she looks at a book about animals in the coral reef. Each piece is part of the large puzzle she is putting together, and she does so with great care. When she is finished, she can't wait to share it with the class. She stands proudly in front of everyone and talks about her project. She, too, is forming her bilingual/biliterate identity by being able to study and share and be accepted in both

FIGURES 7.3 and 7.4
Celia compiled her coral reef poster in both English and Spanish, revealing her bilingual identity.

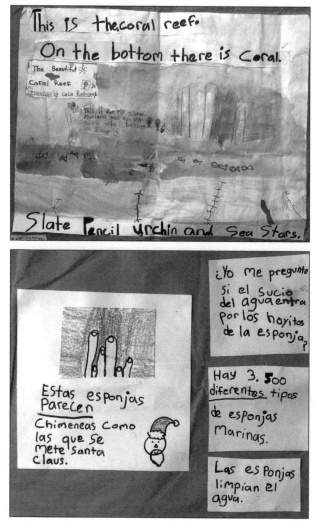

languages. There are times when some of the kids don't understand what she is saying in Spanish, but she takes the time to explain in English as well. Other kids in the crowd quietly translate to the others as she goes. They are all working together to support one another within their community. (See Figures 7.3 and 7.4.)

Pedro and Janice

"I wanna make a poster, Anne," Pedro's voice crawls out from under the big blue hood of his winter jacket.

"Okay." We get inside and Pedro again makes his request. "Can I make my poster now?" At first we don't want to let him work, but he is so persistent that we let him go for it. "Can Janice work with me? We want to do a poster about posters."

"But Janice has other work she needs to finish."

"Please? It won't be long."

"Fine. Go ahead. Get the paper out." Anne, Pedro, and Janice sit down together and start a conversation, in Spanish, about what they want to write. Pedro's first language is Spanish, but his English is stronger. Janice's first language is Spanish and her Spanish is stronger, so we decide to talk in Spanish and write in English. They say, *"Nos encanta hacer afichas."* [We love to make posters.] Anne writes in pencil on the chart paper. They write and reread the text. We go through this process with each sentence until they fill up the chart paper. They take the poster into Brad's room and trace the letters, making bubble letters out of them, adding art and illustrations and glitter. They are so proud of their poster that they can't wait to hang it outside in the hall. So proud that when we try to take it from them to hang it up, they don't want to let go. For almost a month Pedro invites different people to share the poster with. Class after class sits in the hallway as Pedro and Janice read their poster and answer questions. Their teamwork is a way for both of them to form more of their bilingual/biliterate identities by identifying with each other, the two languages, and the outside world. (See Figure 7.5.)

This notion of identity has been important for us to remember. Jim Cummins notes, "They [teachers]

FIGURE 7.5
It's all about writing posters!

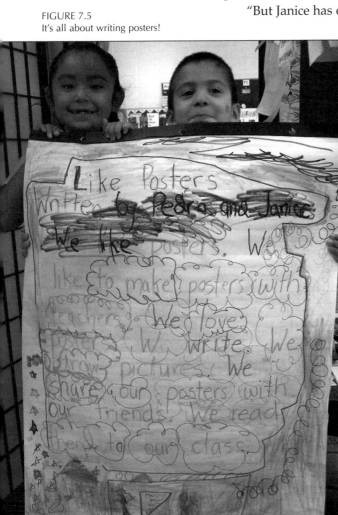

must be proactive and take the initiative to affirm children's linguistic identity . . . encouraging children to write in their mother tongues in addition to the majority school language" (2005).

It is important for us to reject negative attitudes about culturally and linguistically diverse (CLD) students and show them that their cultural capital is accepted, respected, and valued.

WHEN KIDS SHARE, IT LEADS TO INSPIRATION FOR ALL

Getting the kids to share their thinking in a big and bold way also inspires other writers in other grades. This year the kindergarten class did a tour of our rooms and the surrounding hallways because they were initiating their own inquiry projects and wanted ideas about how to publish. One of our students, Stephanie, had done a project on kangaroos and had made a poster with two stuffed kangaroos. For each one she stuffed and stapled two papers together and painted both sides, making a realistic-looking kangaroo. She proudly shared her work while giving a tour to a group of four kindergartners and explained step-by-step how she went about drawing, painting, researching, and writing. A couple of weeks later we were in the library working on mind maps. Stephanie immediately noticed the posters of animals hanging around the room. "Look, Anne! My kangaroo!" she said. The posters of the kindergartners who took the tour with Stephanie imitated her idea of stuffing the animal to make it look three-dimensional. She was so excited she could barely contain herself, and thus the knowledge was shared and spread. Now, by sharing, she had momentum to do more.

Sharing our work is a way for ELLs to explore and play with language and for the entire class to work on a variety of comprehension strategies such as questioning, making connections, and inferring. This whole notion of responding to work is a great way to fine-tune thinking and language writing so children can expand their responses as both their schema and language experiences grow and change. Because sharing and interacting with each other can be overwhelming even in one's native language, we have set up some guidelines to follow to make the experience one of mutual respect for both the author and audience.

We start out with very simple structures and routines for sharing that include oral responses that occur after someone shares. Some of the things kids might say are "I like your research because you wrote a lot," or "I like your project because I learned more about space." As time goes on, responses can be more complicated and can incorporate comprehension strategies such as making connections, questioning, or inferring. When

Jakob inspired me to learn about fish.—Jordan

FIGURE 7.6
Brayan uses a mind map to express his thinking about rain forests.

Alejandra finished sharing a project she had done on tamales, one of her classmates said, "I really liked your poster because it reminded me of when my mom and I made tamales in Mexico." "What kind of connection is that?" we ask. "Text-to-life." It's as simple as that and relevant to those two children, which means they are beginning to internalize what this kind of connection is. It helps them know what this kind of connection truly means. We model different ways to respond as time passes, giving the students a way to access new language structures and new ways to express themselves. Acquiring language implies that an individual listens and watches and often imitates speech and language to understand. Through good modeling the students gain greater access to meaningful language.

"Can I share? When do I get to share?" Brayan keeps asking when it will be time for him to share his mind map on the rain forest. (See Figure 7.6.) He has worked harder on this project than on anything else the entire year. He's so excited that he stops Nell in the hall and translates his thoughts from Spanish to English to share with her. He leaves a note on the principal's message board to come and learn about rain forests. Kids from the other classes flock into the hallway to see what he is so excited about. His mind map, big, beautiful, and full of his new schema, is hanging in the hall for all to see. His enthusiasm reminds us why it is important to make thinking visible. Brayan's pleasure with this particular piece of work is unprecedented. It moves him to share in English with those who don't speak Spanish, which is a breakthrough for him. (See color insert 5.)

The next step is to interact with each other in writing, which has been a great way to promote language and literacy in our classrooms. The community becomes deeply involved in each other's work through presentations of research projects, making connections, asking questions, and writing comments, all of which promotes their English language development. By doing this we help the students bring their work to life. It is also one way we make time for connections to literacy. The key for us is to get ELLs to respond to writing. This is a big part of the writing and publishing process and has become another tool with which they can practice both written and oral language. We have created an environment and sets of routines that allow the kids to be in a comfortable place to share and respond. They serve us in several ways:

- They create a safe zone for sharing writing and receiving constructive criticism.
- They get ELLs excited about publishing their work.
- They let them know that their peers will respond and give positive feedback to their work both orally and in writing.
- They encourage them to share their work with peers and others outside the classroom.
- They help them develop an appreciation for their peers' work and shows them how they can learn from each other.
- They guide them into contributing to other writers by offering and being open to constructive criticism in group or individual settings (both orally and in writing).

While pondering her friend's research about kangaroos Leslie said, "I don't know what to write." We sat down together and read through the project again, looking for things that she liked, learned, or found interesting. As we spoke, we jotted notes on a sticky note. After five minutes we had six sticky notes filled with information about what she liked. "See. There is a lot to write!" She smiled and took the notes, venturing off into a corner with the comment sheet, a clipboard, and her thoughts. It was a great chance for us to interact and allowed her to get her thoughts on paper. Recently we have been experimenting with simply writing our comments on sticky notes and putting them directly onto the work. It has worked really well, because it allows the kids freedom to write more and allows more than one child at a time to respond to the work because they aren't crowded around the response sheet. We also have the kids do drawings to accompany their text as a way to increase comprehension for all. (See Figures 7.7, 7.8, and 7.9.)

A PERSONAL REFLECTION

Delving into this kind of work with the kids has been an enlightening experience for us. Every day the kids come up with new and interesting infor-

FIGURE 7.7 (top)
Alexia notices Pedro's cheetah research in the front lobby of the school. She grabs a pen and a sticky note and reads and responds to Pedro's thinking.

FIGURE 7.8 (bottom)
Oliver writes a response on the comment sheet to a kindergartner about his cheetah research.

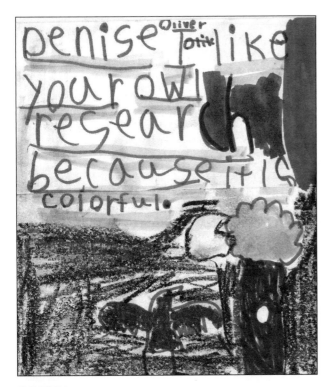

FIGURE 7.9
Oliver responds with art and text to
Denise's owl research.

FIGURE 7.10
Cloe writes a comment to Tristian, her
sister, who did this galaxy project
several years earlier.

mation, often things we don't know anything about. They tend to take their work further than we could ever imagine, particularly with the art. The kids are inspirational to us with their use of art and how they use it to construct meaning. As Peggy Albers notes, ". . . like print-based literacy, meaning making in art is multiple, dynamic, and situated within personal experience" (1997). We hope allowing time for art and the teaching of art keeps us aligned to a transformational way of teaching. Although it may seem cliché to say, we learn more from the kids than we could ever teach them. Luckily we are learning how to take this knowledge and incorporate it into our own teaching and into their classrooms. The environment is truly charged, and the pride in their eyes when they share their work is something we see frequently.

One of the coolest things we've seen is when siblings come back and share and respond to their brother's or sister's work. This happens frequently, and the interactions between the kids are wonderful. "Did you really do this all by yourself?" Cloe asks Tristian of her swirling, glittery solar system inquiry poster. Denise brings both her brother and her sister in to share her beluga whales project, and her older sister is astounded at how creative and how full of information Denise's poster is. Each person takes the time to listen and respond in writing to his or her family member's work.

CHAPTER EIGHT

OUTCOMES: KIDS' WORK ON DISPLAY

We constantly encourage the kids to publish their work, whether it is on the computer or on large chart paper or made into a book. We do this by scaffolding the publishing process so that regardless of where they are with their writing or English-language acquisition, they are able to do it. Consistency in this area has helped our ELL students. Seeing their own stories in published format is inspiring, and the more work that makes it to a completed, published format, the better. Doing this shows the children that their worlds and words matter. If they are publishing for others to see, it inspires them to do great work.

Our publishing tools include a computer; printer; chart paper; white paper; construction paper to make book covers if they want; art supplies for illustration, including paper, paint, chalk, fabric, glue, beads, and glitter; and items such as staplers, yarn, and hole punches. When all of these materials are made available, it gives our children access to their own creativity. They are constantly learning from each other's writing and accompanying art, which truly creates a community of teachers and learners.

Our ELLs have been really successful when given access to a variety of strategies to communicate, and art is a great way for them to express their ideas. This is particularly true for emergent writers. Although their vocabulary and grammar may not yet be as sophisticated as it is in their native language, they are able to add to the words by using art as a means of communication. (See Figure 8.1.)

PUBLISH SO EVERYONE CAN SEE

FIGURE 8.1
Vanessa works on a ladybug poem she is adding to her research.

Publishing and sharing are huge accomplishments, but it is just as important that our classroom provide space for students to display their published works. By displaying work, students can take pride in what they have written. It also gives the other children access to environmental print. The outcomes give kids the opportunity to share and see what their peers are working on, which gives them access to new ideas and information. Students' work needs to be visible even at the beginning writing and publishing stages. A space for displaying work that we like is one that is accessible to the kids so they can read their peers' work and write comments on the comment sheets if they wish. We all know about the importance of publishing and how seeing their work in print and in finished form helps children take ownership of their writing, but what about the rest of the world? A publishing corner/area in a room is crucial for us, but we wonder whether everyone in the building, or for that matter, everyone who walks into our classroom, knows that there is published work there. We like it to be in their faces, screaming out to them, "Read me! I'm here to be read!" We believe that the bigger the better, and if it isn't big, then we put it in a place where everyone can see it and read and respond to it. Putting their work out there helps the students build confidence and pride in their writing. Often we take an easel with kids' work taped to it and put it in the school's front lobby. The first thing people see is our kids' thinking. Next to the work we place a pile of yellow sticky notes and some pens for people to write comments.

When we talk about making thinking visible, we start by using our bulletin boards, filling them with books or posters the kids write. When those are completely covered, we spread the wealth of thinking throughout the building. We think elementary schools are prime real estate for posting children's work. Think about it: for starters there's the hallway outside the classroom, but take a couple of steps down that same hallway, hanging up posters in every nook and cranny you can find. We're fortunate because our ceilings are low and the ceiling tiles graciously accept staples, so even it gets used to make our kids' writing visible. As the wall space is filled, we creep around the corner into the bathroom. This is a great place to hang kids' work. We end up reading everything—we can't help it. Plus it spices up what are typically plain gray walls and stalls. Collaborate with the media specialist to find space in the library where the entire school community will have access to the kids' writing. This communal space is perfect for sharing important work. In our building the cafeteria is a great place to post projects as well, and some years the walls are lined with research projects and narratives. Kids pass their time munching peanut-butter sandwiches or slurping macaroni noodles and gazing upward, reading each other's work. It is also a source of pride for the budding writers. Once they see their work going up in the hallways and other parts of the building, they begin to constantly push for more of it to be posted where the whole school can see. Not only is it a positive self-esteem booster, but it allows them to bring in a variety of audiences such as family (for example, cousins in other grades who notice their family member's work on the door to gym), other teachers, the principal, kids from other grades, and visitors. The audience is suddenly broadened beyond the students in the classroom.

EVERYONE PUBLISHES OFTEN TO BUILD A REPERTOIRE

Our anecdotal evidence shows that the more kids take their research to the publishing stage, the more they are able to internalize all the steps in the process. The kids who have practiced the steps in the research and writing process and know what's coming are better able to reach that stage of independence we're aiming for. For this reason, we closely guide our kids early on to get to the publishing stage quickly.

There are unlimited ways in which kids can publish. The key is to make publishing fun and exciting and allow time for more learning through the process. Discovery happens along the way. New information is added if kids come across something they think they missed. Kids know they can always add to their thinking if they have more to say. There is no one way to publish that is best, because all students have different artistic styles. Again, the ideas for how to publish pieces come from the children and what they know or are interested in. We can provide models for ideas, but frequently the kids modify them and come up with better ones. We not only let them, but encourage them. As with writing, we see publishing as a process that allows students to show their thinking and work through ideas. Publishing also allows for:

- meaning making;
- making learning matter;
- owning knowledge together;
- the differentiation of outcomes;
- scaffolding through a gradual release of responsibility;
- kids to show their varied interests;
- the ability to guide students through modeling and mini-lessons;
- the teacher to base instruction on student approximations;
- the opportunity to add to our class pot of information.

IDEAS OF WAYS KIDS CAN PUBLISH

The following outcomes have been great ways for our kids to make their thinking explode:

Starting Small and Going Big

A big sheet of blank paper may be overwhelming for some kids when they are beginning to illustrate or write words for their research. Something that has worked well is starting really small and allowing the kids to build from it. A sticky note with an "I learned" attached to a small image the kids have drawn acts a starting point. The kids can draw first to help generate some words, as Javier did with his thresher shark inquiry, then write. (See Figure 8.2.) Many kids go back and forth between drawing first and writing first; the text supports the image and the image supports the text.

Often we continue to give them a small piece of white paper for an illustration that relates to the text on their sticky note. The sticky note, which works as a caption, is attached to the paper and is glued to a larger sheet of thick paper. This creates a larger canvas for the kids to write and draw what they know, what they wonder, and what really excites or interests them.

One sticky note can turn into a project the size of a door. The kids take the large squares of thick white paper and glue them to their current piece, illustrate it according to what they've learned or wondered about, and then add text on either a sticky note or a larger sentence strip.

When the kids are given time, they are difficult to stop and their projects can become enormous, filled with nonfiction features such as comparisons, close-ups, labels, and captions. (See Figures 8.3 and 8.4.)

What It Looks Like

Kids take notes using different-colored sticky notes.

They draw images to represent their notes.

They stick them on a small piece of construction paper.

They add illustrations.

They go back to do more note taking, which leads them to make their sheet bigger.

They add another piece of construction paper and keep adding notes.

It is an ongoing process that sometimes starts as one tiny square and ends up being gigantic and eye-catching.

FIGURE 8.2
Javier started with one small sticky note, illustrated, and went from there. Framing his poster are the class's responses to his research.

Published Notes

Another great way for kids to show their thinking is to organize their notes on their published piece of work or even next to it for the entire world to see. Some kids choose to complete their exploration of the topic by presenting giant notes they have gathered. Other kids like to continue with their project by making what they have learned come to life through symbolic representations. After reading and exploring a topic, notes can be written or art can be done. It doesn't matter which one comes first. Kent spent time organizing his notes, which came first for him. He moved notes and drew arrows to connect pieces of information (see color insert 6). Sometimes these projects

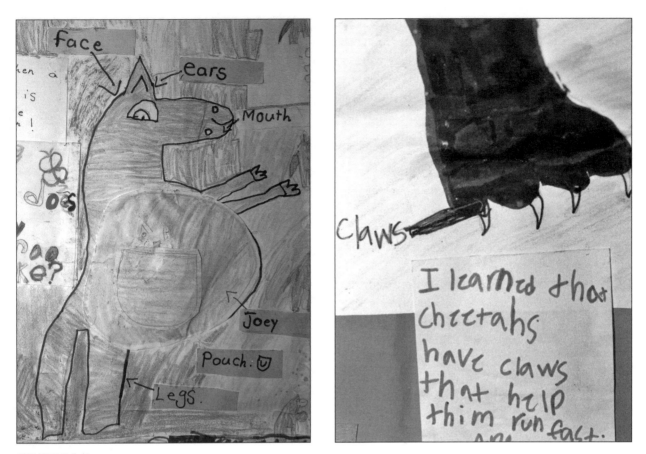

FIGURE 8.3 (left)
Edith labels her kangaroo to make it more comprehensible to others.

FIGURE 8.4 (right)
Ana draws a close-up of a cheetah claw to emphasize its claws.

can take quite a long time. Kent worked more than a month on his King Crab Adventures. The entire time his project was in progress we kept it out and visible so it wouldn't be forgotten. Sometimes Kent wanted to work on something else, so in the meantime he wrote a comic book, read, and did some other writing. Just when we thought he was finished, he would find some more information to write or draw.

"I'm going to switch these [sticky notes] and put [the] *shelter* [sticky note] next to *shell*. I'm going to draw an arrow," he began to tell us. "I'm going to switch *jointed* and *legs* so it says 'jointed legs.' *Shell* is sort of the same as *exoskeleton* and *shelter*, and it's the same as body, too. The body has exoskeleton and shell and shelter. The body has all these parts. I put *claws* next to *sharp* and next to *spike* because the claws are very sharp and the spikes are, too. The body has no bones. What's next? What do they eat, maybe shrimp?" When he finally finished, he shared it with the fourth graders who were doing research in the library.

What It Looks Like

Kids explore a topic of interest.
Information is gathered and written in notes.

Different-colored sticky notes are stuck on a giant note-taking chart.
Illustrations accompany text with notes.
Art is made big.
Notes are attached to a poster.

Posters

David is really interested in sharks, which is great, but there are a lot of different kinds. After a conversation about his books and the many species, he decides to focus on one—the whale shark. Together we start the research by looking at the images we have of whale sharks. While we are looking and talking about the images, we notice some captions that go with them, and we read and reread those. As we are reading and looking, we talk about what we see. Together at the table in the library we talk about what is interesting and might be important information to share with the class. We write some of his thinking on a sticky note, and he transfers it to a small strip of paper. Later he will add these sentence strips to his poster. We talk about how you just write what you notice, just like we did in our conversation. He is left to start writing. He is talking to himself, recapping what he is seeing and then writing it down on his note-taking sheet. He knows that he can put those words he's written into sentences that make sense. Within a short time David has a lot of his thinking written down in note form. We talk about how we can make his notes into sentences by pretending he is telling kids what he learned and his wonderings. Within one hour we have chosen a topic, narrowed it down, read and observed for information (which generated even more questions), written notes, and begun to put notes into sentences for publishing. Next time we will glue them on some poster paper and add illustrations. David can see the success he's already had and has momentum to keep his thinking going next time.

What It Looks Like
We gather images and text as resources.
We write information on sticky notes.
We put sticky notes on a note sheet ("I learned"/"I wonder").
The student writes sentences and illustrates. If strips of paper are
    used, they are glued where the student wants them. This takes
    some organization.
The student writes in pencil and self-edits. Another student edits, and
    the teacher does a final edit.
The student goes over words in black marker and illustrates.
The student can cut out words and glue them on the paper.
The student shares and publishes for all to see and read.

Modify Text on Posters to Make It BIG

Some kids like to make their words big and full of color. The information with large words and huge images to support the writing or vice versa has a great effect on the reader. When the kids show their thinking big, we get a better glimpse of who they are (see color insert 7). We sit down with them on the floor and talk about making big letters. With a pencil we scribe some of their thoughts to get them started. The kids watch us getting started and are eager to get going themselves. Because they are going immediately into publishing, we have them use pencils so they can erase if needed. We expect published pieces to have standard conventions. When they are making their big posters, kids use pencils to put their words down and then self-edit. The piece is peer-edited, and we look at the writing and give a final edit. That way we can write the words that are not conventionally written on a sticky note and let them fix them. Even with the big words we encourage kids to add symbolic representations to make the text more comprehensible. Sometimes they have a big image of what the writing is about or smaller ones using the kind of image frames mentioned above.

What It Looks Like

We use large sheets of paper.
We model writing large letters.
We model coloring words.
We use a pencil or highlighter to make big letters.
We use a marker to go over the pencil.
We color words.

Poetry

After a student has gathered information on a subject, another possible outcome is poetry. To help them get started, we hold a page from a cut-apart book about the rain forest and talk about how we are going to play with words. The page we have taped to the chart paper is filled with animals and plants. Next we read and reread some of the text and talk about what we see. Immediately we begin to write what we see and have read. We like to reread the text a few times, stopping occasionally to make some comments about the text and images on the page. We begin a conversation with the kids about which words to write. Soon we have a few pages of text with images from the pages of the book we've chosen. Next to each piece of text we draw a small symbolic representation: "leafy canopy, howler monkeys leaping, looping liana vines" are some examples of the text we've chosen to write. We write some words together, some alone, and some in sentences. Then we read and illustrate.

We have relearned poetry as a genre related to nonfiction inquiry. In fact it is the perfect genre for such writing and for ELLs to develop and practice new vocabulary and grammatical structures in context. It is also a way for them to make literacy connections from one form of writing to another.

What It Looks Like

We read a lot of poetry to start and develop schema about poetry.

We read from cut-apart books with vibrant images to generate vocabulary, language structures, and mental images.

We write text that is interesting on chart paper.

We draw symbolic representations for text on chart paper.

Using notes and images, we brainstorm rich language syntax and vocabulary.

We discuss phrases that convey meaning or information gathered.

We act as scribes or have children write.

We write directly on large chart paper or on sentence strips to glue on later.

We draw symbolic representations on paper to reflect the poem and our knowledge.

FIGURE 8.5
Ansel creates poetry about tornadoes through looking at images and generating descriptive language.

Later (as a group project or individually):

We use picture books to generate descriptive language.

We model how to brainstorm language by browsing through the book and writing down the words that come to mind.

We use the vocabulary to model how to write a poem.

We release kids to work alone or in small groups.

We have kids brainstorm words and write/scribe on a long strip of paper.

Kids write poems using their list of words.

Kids edit and then publish poems on large chart paper. (See Figure 8.5.)

Mobile

The kids use an organizer with two columns like the giant note-taking chart, which are labeled "I Learned" and "I Wonder." Topics of study and inquiry are open to the kids, and we encourage them to explore and discover and wonder. Kids love to make mobiles, and as a bonus, it frees up wall space for other thinking. After kids have read and gathered information through their "I Learned," "I Wonder" chart, they put their notes into sentences. We usually sit down and have a conversation about what was learned and what is written in their notes. Using strips of paper, we scribe what is said by the child with whom we're working exactly as they talk, while putting their words into conventional syntax. With another strip of paper we draw lines to represent each word. The kids then copy what was scribed, which are their words, onto the other sheet. This is a way to scaffold this process, and the more the kids experience what it takes to explore a topic and publish it, the more quickly they are able to do it more independently. Sometimes kids have written their notes into sentences. We then have small squares of white paper for them to draw their illustrations as they relate to the text. These small sheets act like captions telling about the illustration. We take each strip of paper with text and illustration and glue it on construction paper. Each sheet of construction paper has information on each side. When all the notes are written and illustrated and glued on construction paper, we help the kids plan their mobile so it balances. We lay it out on the floor and plan it. Then with a hole punch we make our holes to put the yarn through and tie a knot. If the mobile gets too big, we simply cut off excess construction paper to bring the size down. We have the kids share their thinking, others respond to it, and then we hang it up for all to see and read. Creating mobiles also internalizes a means of sharing what you are excited about. Alma's monkey mobile was a great teaching tool, because it presented an opportunity for a mini-lesson on captions. She wanted to print photos of monkeys from some on-line resources to include in her mobile. Our conversation about how to share with the readers what the images represented led to her writing captions for each photo.

What It Looks Like

A student gathers resources and takes notes.

The teacher helps the student by scribing.

The teacher draws lines to represent each word a student said on a thin strip of white paper.

The student writes from sticky notes to a thin strip of white paper.

A larger sheet of white paper is placed above the thin strip for a symbolic representation to be drawn. Thin strips of paper become captions.

The student colors an image to go with each caption.

The student adds nonfiction features of her choice.

The student glues her information onto construction paper.

The student creates a mobile by punching holes and using yarn to connect each sheet of paper.

The mobile is shared and displayed.

Big Books

Big Books are ideal outcomes because children are familiar with them. They have experienced them in class through read-alouds, and by reading them on their own and with the library media specialist. For those children who like to make books, they are a good way to make their thinking visible. We like to do this as a shared writing experience to introduce it. Depending on our topic, we bring the kids up close around the easel and chart paper. For example, if we are studying insects, we have our objective written out as, "We are going to make a Big Book from what we know about insects."

After telling the kids the objective, we begin with a think-pair-share. We tell the kids to think about what they know about insects. After pairing with a friend, they share with the group. We simply write down what they say, draw and color a quick image to represent their thinking, and if necessary, put their words into conventional syntax. "I know insects have three body parts," says David. We write, "Insects have three body parts." Alexia adds, "Insects have an abdomen." We write that and put Alexia's name next to it. José Carlos says, "Insects have a thorax and a head, too." We write that. You can see how quickly we have three chart pages filled with writing and small images to represent the text. Now with a strip of white construction paper we show the kids what they are going to do. We model choosing what someone said, and then we write it on our paper. We say we know how to spell the words because they are right here. We remind the kids of conventions by saying, "We know how to begin a sentence, and we know how to end a sentence, and we know how to leave spaces between our words."

After we write, we take another paper cut into a square or rectangle and begin drawing an image to represent the text. The image we draw is not complex, just a quick sketch to show the kids what they are going to do. We say, "You're going to make your drawing beautiful because you'll have more time." Now we take our text that we wrote on our sentence strip and our image and glue them onto the construction paper. "Look how easy this is!" we say to the group. By now they are eager to get going, so we release them one by one. As the kids are released, we hand them a clipboard, marker, strips of paper for writing and drawing, and a large sheet for their page. Some kids may write directly from our shared writing, but others may want to write something different or new. We let them. This is a great way to build a community of thinkers, because we are creating an informational text together. Soon our classroom library has another informational text that we wrote in class that has nonfiction features and is very comprehensible.

What It Looks Like

Using large sheets of white construction paper and either notebook paper or sentence strips, the students can organize and write their information in a Big Book. For emergent speakers the teacher can act as a scribe.

We make it a shared writing experience.

The teacher models writing and drawing.

Kids are gradually released to work.

The kids can organize the book as they like. We provide them with samples of Big Books that are nonfiction.

This is an opportunity to integrate through a mini-lesson some nonfiction conventions such as a table of contents, bold text, labels, and captions.

Schema Chart Across the Curriculum

We head over to the computer and open up the word processor. By drawing two rectangles we have our paper divided into two parts. We make our rectangles so they are placed on top of each other, and we leave room beneath each one to write a sentence or two with our objective. For this lesson we are studying air and weather, so we type, "My schema about air and weather is growing and changing." We underline the words *schema* and *air* and *weather.* This sentence is followed by the sentence frames "I learned _____." "I wonder _____." We pull the kids close to the easel with our enlarged schema chart posted on it. Above our enlarged schema chart we have our objective written: "We are writing and illustrating our schema about air and weather. We are making our thinking about air and weather visible."

Pointing to our objective we read it together. Thinking aloud we begin modeling what we know about air and weather and what we did in our last investigation. We think aloud about our recent investigation, which was to see what would happen to a balloon placed on a bottle filled with cold water versus one with hot water in it. "Let's draw what happened in our investigation." Quickly we draw the two bottles with the balloons. The kids see and hear us thinking about what to draw. They see us making one bottle filled with red water to symbolize hot water and the other with blue water to symbolize cold water. We stop there, but continue to think about what to do to finish our drawing. We then move to our sentence frame "I learned _____." "What did we learn?" we say aloud. The kids, who have been sitting somewhat quietly, are having a difficult time not sharing. Quickly we write a sentence, "I learned cold water didn't move the balloon." We stop modeling and ask the kids, "What did you see us doing?" On our chart paper we write the sentence frame "I saw you _____." We underline the word *saw* and draw a little picture of some kids looking at the chart. These symbolic representations are done very quickly to aid comprehension of the text. Next is a quick think-pair-share about what they saw us doing. Then we have the kids briefly share what they saw or noticed. We write their names next to their observations to validate their ideas and build confidence. "Show us with your thumbs if you know what to do." Now all the kids have their thumbs up. We release them by looking at them one by one. They get up, get a clipboard, and find a place to begin working. Once they are all working, we get up and confer with them, scaffolding by scribing where needed, drawing lines to represent their words if needed, or encouraging them in their drawings. After the kids have time to complete their schema charts, we group back together and share some of our thinking. Their schema charts are then posted in either the room or the hall.

This chart is a great way for the kids to synthesize their thinking on just about any topic we are investigating as a group or as an individual inquiry. (See Appendix.)

What It Looks Like

We draw two rectangles on a sheet of paper.

Beneath the top rectangle we write a sentence about our schema in context and underline key vocabulary.

We make an enlarged schema sheet for modeling.

We model how to write and illustrate using writing routines.

We release the students, share, and post the charts.

Date: Gelaldo

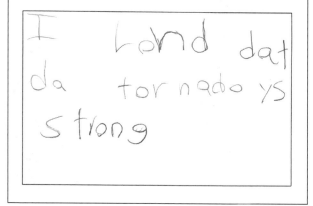

My **schema** about **wind** is growing and changing. I learned...

I Lohnd dat da tornado ys strong

FIGURE 8.6
Schema charts help scaffold kids' thinking and writing.

Matrices

Matrices can be another way we learn from each other. An example from an insect study is a matrix for insect attributes. After the kids have started their inquiry projects on insects, we get together to start our matrix. We make six or seven columns, decide what insects we should explore, and write them horizontally at the top. We have volunteers draw pictures to represent each one so we have text and an image of many insects across the top. A long sheet of butcher paper works best for this. With strips of different-colored construction paper we begin adding information as we come across it. We use different-colored strips of paper to make each piece of thinking stand out. Kent found out mosquitoes have long tubes to suck blood. We write that on a piece of construction paper with a little picture that he drew of a mosquito sucking blood. Adding an image really helps the kids connect to the text they have written.

FIGURE 8.7
Kids categorize their thinking using matrices.

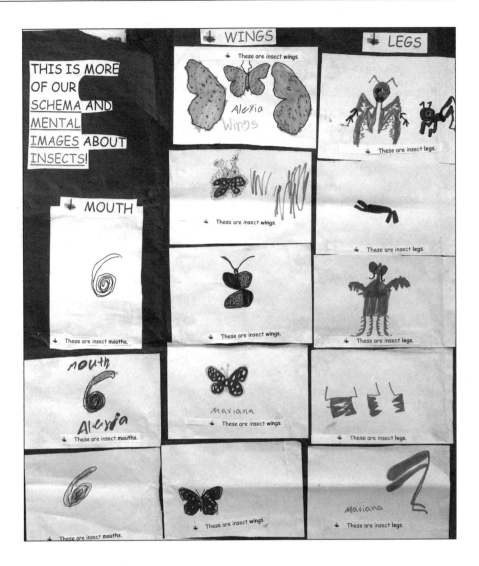

What It Looks Like

Topics are organized on a large piece of butcher paper in columns and rows, and images accompany headings.

Information is written on strips of construction paper to be glued or taped on the matrix.

Symbolic representations created by the kids accompany text on strips.

Comics Based on Inquiry

Some kids like to present their information in a different way from most people, and making a comic strip to show what you know is one of them. (See Figure 8.8.) This works best if the kids have had some experience reading comics, so we have a lot in our classroom library. When kids show

FIGURE 8.8
Jamie used a comic to make his thinking about Aurora Borealis visible. He included nonfiction features such as arrows, labels, and a map to make his comic very informative.

an interest in reading them, we work with them in small groups or one on one and give them a mini-lesson. The comic format can be as big or small as the kids' desire. Kids have drawn themselves as narrators being on an adventure and coming across new information. All the kids do is draw themselves talking, with bubbles around the text. They can add a fictional twist to their information, too, like traveling in time or becoming bigger or smaller like in The Magic School Bus series.

What It Looks Like

We get lots of comic books for the classroom.
We read comics aloud.
We talk about comic book features.
We model making nonfiction comics.

Murals with Sticky Notes

Murals can be fun because they bring together the entire community to work on one project about any given topic. Brad's group had been studying ocean life and Anne's group had been studying insects, so we got together to make one huge mural to show our thinking about both topics. Anne's group worked on the land and Brad's on the water.

We did this by taking huge pieces of paper and laying them on the floor. Each child found a section to work on. We gathered the kids together for a

FIGURE 8.9
Insects and ocean life interact in this collaborative mural. Captions and labels were used by the students to add more information.

conversation about the topic. After a think-pair-share, we wrote what kids knew about the topic. The kids' words were later written by them on different-colored sticky notes to put on the mural. We modeled using frames such as, "I learned _____," "This is a _____," "I wonder _____?" and "Wow!" The kids worked on writing their thinking down, and when they were ready took a spot on the mural to make their illustrations big and beautiful. They added nonfiction features to their illustrations. Because they were working together, there was a lot of talking. They fed off of each other and all of the information in the room, such as other inquiries and the word walls. It turned into a collage of color and text. (See Figure 8.9.)

What It Looks Like

We place a large sheet of paper on the floor.

We gather sticky notes.

We link thinking to one area of study (e.g., insects).

We have a class discussion about what the group knows.

We write what the group knows on sticky notes and glue them onto the paper.

We illustrate and write text.

EQUAL TIME FOR ALL

We keep mental notes and sometimes write down who has published. We want to give equally of our time and guidance. This can be a struggle, because some of the kids who really call out for attention can take all our time if we are not careful. We have become more conscious of balancing our time and doing our best to spend equal amounts of time with each student.

As we experiment with different forms of publishing with our ELLs, we keep in mind what sorts of things would benefit them. Publishing should do the following:

Provide opportunities to develop new vocabulary.

Use scaffolded language to get to meaning.

Limit immediate stress of standard structure in the short term.

Develop oral language skills.

Have texts that are often directly linked to images.

Give ELLs an opportunity to show their thinking through varying levels of text and art.

Become a resource for other children in the classroom library.

Be looked at as a way to authentically assess their work.

Help make their thinking visible.

Build schema.

Help organize and distribute thinking into groups or sections that make it more comprehensible.

Synthesize thinking and learning.

Be something kids can work on together and learn from each other.

Allow for conversations with each other.

Promote art as a valid means of expression and meaning making.

Artifacts Are Valuable Resources

We also like to keep artifacts. For a long time we were conflicted about what to do with all our students' displays of thinking. As the kids get their thinking routines internalized and explore, read, write, and publish their inquiries, space becomes an issue. We have to take their thinking down to replace it with newly published posters, mind maps, and books. But what happens to all that great inquiry and information, and the responses from kids and adults? After wondering, "Should we send it home? Should we keep it?" we decided we could do both.

We decided to keep it for a few reasons. We save the kids' work and use it to teach the following year. In the library, Nell uses kids' past work to teach nonfiction features and other features of an inquiry endeavor. She starts from the first day of school using their thinking to keep the momentum of exploring topics going. We also save work to show other teachers what these kids are capable of doing if we just let them. The kids' work turns into what we call "The Archives." The Archives are boxes and boxes of rolled-up mind maps, giant maps from content study, student posters of inquiry, and narratives as well as books and word walls. We have even started collaborating with Anne Goudvis to convert her basement into The Archives. It is bursting with life. Again, we take out our digital camera to document the kids' thinking and so we can use it in slide shows and presentations (both ours and the kids'), and so we can print various copies of the same piece. Our computers contain files and files of images of all that amazing work. Being able to take their work around to different schools, labs, and conferences has been an inspiration to us all. Rolling up the pieces, labeling them on the outside, and storing them in tubs preserves them fairly well. We strongly advise against laminating them, because in the end it doesn't really save them, and as Brad says, "Would you laminate a Monet?" It is artwork, so we treat it as such. Some folks ask us what the kids say about not taking their work home. When they know it is because we are sharing it with others, they are fascinated. As they get older, they see us use their stuff to teach the first graders. They are excited and filled with pride. We keep their work alive.

A PERSONAL REFLECTION

Publishing can be made into a long and arduous process where six- and seven-year-old kids are writing, editing, rewriting, editing again, rewriting, copying, editing, rewriting, getting a headache, losing concentration and interest, and finally giving up. At least this is what we have seen when publishing becomes "The Final Product," instead of a piece of the process. The idea that there even exists a final product is something we go round and round about. If we are promoting a transformational style of learning, is anything really ever finished? Don't we just keep questioning and learning in the cycle of life and knowledge? Because these questions have arisen for us, we approach publishing with the idea that it is part of the writing process that happens often and is a work in progress.

CHAPTER NINE

INVESTIGATING CONTENT TOPICS

. . . We have also found that classes in school that are highly interactive, emphasizing student problem-solving and discovery learning through thematic experiences across the curriculum are likely to provide the kind of social setting for natural language acquisition to take place, simultaneously with academic and cognitive development. (Thomas and Collier 1995)

FIGURE 9.1
Miguel and Jaime help show how tall a giraffe can be by standing next to the kindergartners' giraffe.

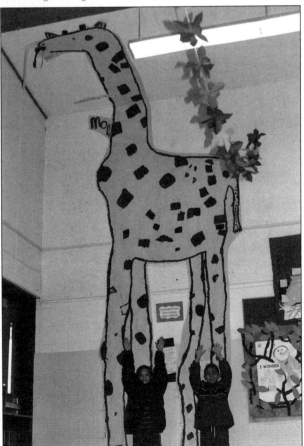

"What are you doing?" Lynn, our principal, asks José Carlos and Kent, when she sees them in the hallway with several bowls of paint.

"We're building Mount Fuji." Her eyebrows go up as she looks at the newspaper covering the floor.

"Why?" she asks.

"We're studying Japan, and Mount Fuji is in Japan," José Carlos answers. "And later I'm going to study how to build a volcano and make it explode!" He grins. While an exploding volcano in the hallway isn't a principal's dream, she knows that his excitement cannot be contained. A few weeks later he is sharing his project with her under the cherry trees that hang from the ceiling.

When we say we surround ourselves with content, we mean it. Everyone knows what we are studying because our rooms are drenched in whatever it is. One of our colleagues in second grade, Sue, transforms her room into an ocean habitat, with jellyfish hanging from the ceiling and tidal pools in the corner during the Australia unit. The kindergarten teacher, Kristen, hangs an orca that stretches the length of the cafeteria during their unit on Antarctica. It has turned into a healthy competition—who can make their units the most exotic? By submersing ourselves in the content the level of comprehensible input goes up. The more we see, the more we understand. (See Figure 9.1.)

We thread content and areas of study throughout the day and surround our students with the themes we are studying. Content is present in literacy, ESL, social studies or science, and sometimes even math. This has worked well with our ELL students because it gives them the opportunity to work on different parts of a topic during different parts of the day. It is also a wonderful way to open up new areas of the curriculum for exploration in their own inquiry projects. Integrating the content has helped build a launching pad for fresh, interesting, and surprising inquiry projects by the students.

ENDURING UNDERSTANDINGS AND ESSENTIAL QUESTIONS

We use enduring understandings and essential questions rather than factoids to organize and frame our content inquiry units. Enduring understandings are concepts developed around the curriculum and district and state standards. They are ideas that connect with the real world, with different cultures, and with people. Whereas standards are often focused on students learning facts, enduring understandings and essential questions are broader. They form the framework around a unit. For example, a standard for social studies might be "Students understand the history of social organization in various societies" whereas an enduring understanding might be something like "The beliefs and actions of people determine their culture." These understandings help us stay focused on knowledge rather than on factoids. Although being familiar with the sequence of history is important, it can often turn into memorization of facts and may or may not be culturally relevant, depending on the perspective from which it is presented. The enduring understanding allows for further exploration of the why and how. When facts are generated, it is extremely hard to compare and contrast, and to analyze and critique information and learning. By focusing on and developing what's really important, we have been able to set frameworks that drive our instruction and best serve the needs of our students. In essence we hope that by understanding the big ideas of why we study something, the kids will want to learn and wonder more and seek out the information.

To guide these big pictures we develop the essential questions that connect with day-to-day life. If we were studying communities and their cultures, an example of an essential question might be "How does weather affect people in different communities?"

IT CAN BE AS SIMPLE AS MAKING CONNECTIONS

We make connections throughout our areas of study as well. Connecting our learning and using our background knowledge helps us think more deeply. It is really about taking our new learning and linking it to past learning. "Remember when we studied Mexico and Japan last year? Well, Australia is an island, too—a really big one!" or "Remember how we talked about our community? Now we're going to look at communities in Japan, too." Making a connection helps the kids make sense of new information even if it is factual. We are always thinking about connecting content day to day and year to year. It can be as simple as comparing Japanese volcanoes with Alaskan seismic activity. The point is to get the kids excited and enthusiastic about discovery through content.

As we go through the year, we also maintain focus on organizing learning and outcomes so they are connected to one another and generate deeper and more meaningful thinking. Through writing and art we are synthesizing our learning and thinking. Metacognition is a big part of this.

I like to read the book so I can see a lot of information, like stuff we studied in first grade, like volcanoes and tsunamis.—Brandon

We think about our thinking, which internalizes learning at extraordinarily deep levels. This is important for ELLs, because it gives what they are learning meaning. It helps them construct a world that is relevant to them and that makes sense. The more deeply the information penetrates the mind, the easier it is for them to learn their new language and still be exposed to interesting and exciting content.

The idea of linking everything together is a powerful tool, because it keeps us thinking about our curriculum, our kids' needs, and our delivery of material. It sends us on a quest for better materials, and it forces us to learn more about these subjects than we ever imagined we would have to.

MORE SCHEMA!

Regardless of the area of the day, we always remind the kids that they are building their schema. It is always at the forefront of our minds, because it is so important that they are learning, not just memorizing facts. Mario is an intermediate English speaker and decides he wants to write about Alaska. He is working on a schema chart. He has the language structure in front of him: "My schema about Alaska is changing and growing. I learned _____." He eagerly asks where Alaska is on the globe. When we show him, his eyes light up. "Hey, it's on North America!" He's so excited. "Yes," we tell him. "Isn't that on the continent I drew last week?" he asks. He runs over to the Alaska content word wall and points to the card with the word *continent*, and his drawing on it, which he had done several days earlier. He had chosen North America because he remembered that it was a continent from our studies on Mexico. He had diligently sat on the floor copying the map from the globe; he even used the same colors. It took him only a few moments to make a connection that allowed him to internalize his learning. Alaska is in North America. He learned the word and figured out where it was in relation to his home and other places in the world we had studied. Later that week he began looking more and more at the globe and asked if we had any other maps. We took out atlases and opened up all the maps on the wall. His fascination grew as he began to learn that there is much more out there than he had thought. He began drawing maps in his journal, copying them from atlases, and labeling the names of the countries in English. He spent weeks using his free-choice time to make the maps. They were now his.

THE NITTY-GRITTY: WHEN DO WE DO WHAT?

Two questions come up over and over: When do you do what? and How do you know what is appropriate for different times of the day? This really depends on the kind of program in your school, but if we were to break down our day to explain how we think about organizing thematic units, it might look something like this.

Literacy

During literacy we focus on building literacy skills and addressing our curriculum while threading content into our teaching. If, for example, we are studying Australia, we might do read-alouds about Australia, give the kids access to texts about Australia in case they want to study it, and work on any number of comprehension strategies while using pictures of or text about Australia. We are still working on building literacy and at the same time bringing the content into the classroom.

Our literacy block is also an excellent opportunity for the kids to further explore topics about a content unit through an inquiry. Brandon became obsessed with volcanoes. His obsession was derived from a story we read about volcanoes in Mexico, the unit we were working on at the time. To work on his questioning strategies we took a book filled with images of active volcanoes from around the world. Immediately his mind was filled with questions. "What is the red stuff?" "How does a volcano explode?" "Where are they?" "Do they hurt people?" In the past we might not have realized how important these wonderings are. Now we capitalize on them because this is something that matters. We pointed out what he was doing and helped him generate an entire list of questions. He became the expert on volcanoes, and we brought his work into our unit on Mexico and later into our unit on Japan. He had access to vocabulary because during ESL we made a picture dictionary filled with words associated with volcanoes. In science we did an experiment where the kids built volcanoes and observed them as they exploded. Things naturally became connected. This kind of connecting opens up a child's mind to discovery because he or she sees that the topic is something new, yet at the same time is connected to something we are studying. We explicitly pointed out that schema building was happening. All of this occurred at the same time he was practicing reading, writing, and note taking. (See Figure 9.2.)

FIGURE 9.2
Paint explodes in a gush of lava.

The lesson framework we use to plan has been developed by Columbine Elementary faculty and staff over the last several years. It has been a great tool for all of us to organize our thinking and be strategic in our planning.

One lesson we might work on focuses on comprehension strategies. We can weave content into literacy and practice reading for meaning and note taking, which will later help us with our inquiries. It might look something like the lesson outlined on pages 129–130.

ESL

We have different levels of ESL classes for children who receive native language literacy. Instead of teaching a scripted program, we take this time to build vocabulary and language structures for the students that are related directly to the content we are studying. We might play games that build vocabulary about the content, such as a bingo game with pictures and labels of animals from Alaska or a form of Pictionary using content vocabulary, or make ABC books about the geography of Australia, or have the kids create content word walls so that when they are writing in English, they have access to text that makes sense to them. ABC books are used to build vocabulary, synthesize our thinking, show our new schema, and get new ideas for inquiries (see pages 131–132).

For more advanced students this is a time when we introduce the inquiry process in English. These are the students who are receiving native language literacy and have already begun to build schema and practiced language structures in their L1 (first, primary, or heritage language) that allows them to comprehend what is going on and participate. We point out similarities and differences in language structure and syntax between Spanish and English, which later helps them be more aware of the relationship between their two languages.

We also take ESL time to develop vocabulary through the use of meaningful print. When we say "meaningful print," we are talking about text that children can relate to and make connections with. Vygotsky keeps reminding us, context, context, context. Text that is not attached to something of significance for an ELL might as well not even exist. Often, we teachers don't realize that vocabulary tests or rote memorization of words do not help our ELLs, because they have no image in their minds of what those words mean. Having kids copy words that they don't understand and in a setting where the words are out of context is not helpful. However, creating a space with meaningful print through things such as content word walls, news walls, magazines, other kids' work, books, and shared writings has helped our ELLs access text that otherwise would be unfamiliar to them.

Unit: Mexico	Area of Study: Geography and People

Lesson (learning focus): Determining meaning through nonfiction conventions	Time Frame: This is an activity that can be done over and over.

Content Objective:
Students will be able to read nonfiction texts about the people of Mexico for meaning and take notes.

Language Objective:
Students will be able to gather information through printed text and/or pictures, building schema and content vocabulary.

Outcome:
Students will read and take notes and share.

Enduring Understanding:
Climate affects how people live and act within a community.

Essential Question:
How do different climates affect lifestyles in Mexico?

Type of Lesson:
- ☐ Literacy Block L1 ✔   Mixed Group ___   ESL L2 ___
- ☐ ESL L2 (outside literacy block)
- ☐ Integrated Whole Group

Essential Vocabulary: schema, nonfiction	Core Vocabulary: bold print, italics, labels, table of contents	Extended Vocabulary: index, captions

Activate Prior Knowledge: Through modeling using a nonfiction text (study print or book) on Mexico, teacher models and talks about how to read for meaning.	Post-Assessment: Children will share notes taken from study print.

Materials:
nonfiction texts (books, magazines, or study prints); sticky notes; pens

Description of Lesson:
1. Gather high-quality images/accessible text.
2. Teacher models note taking (five-minute mini-lesson).
3. Kids watch and listen.
4. Teacher thinks aloud and models making mistakes.
5. Teacher models strategies to get through difficulties.
6. Write information and questions derived through looking at pictures and/or reading text on sticky notes.
7. Think aloud where to place sticky note.
8. Review with kids: "What did you see me doing?" for two minutes; write it down.
9. Think-pair-share with a neighbor, two minutes.
10. Teacher listens in on conversations.
11. Ask for responses; write and post on the left side.
12. Gradually release students to do what you did. Teacher confers.
13. Kids can work for fifteen–thirty minutes.
14. Regroup and share some of what we learned.

Remember, this is a lesson that will be done over and over with different materials. Students usually can't wait to get started, especially when they see all the cool books, magazines, and images that they can search through.

Differentiation:
This lesson can be easily differentiated based on reading stages and language stages by providing a variety of materials and accessible texts. Students can take notes by doing drawings, labeling, or writing more complex sentences. Teacher should model all of the ways the children can take notes. Teacher can also scaffold.

Enhanced Learning Strategies:
- ❑ Preview/review vocabulary.
- ❑ Preview/review objective.
- ❑ Use realia.
- ❑ Think-pair-share.
- ❑ Use guarded vocabulary.
- ❑ Use slowed and articulated speech.
- ❑ Use sentence/language frames.
- ❑ Post objectives.
- ❑ Use visuals.
- ❑ Use graphic organizers.

Resource List/Bibliography:
any of the nonfiction texts on the bibliography; study prints; *Time for Kids*

Unit: Mexico	Area of Study: Mexico

Lesson (learning focus): ABC book	Time Frame: Several weeks

Content Objective:
Students will demonstrate an understanding of varying content concepts by publishing a book.

Language Objective:
Students will be able to write and orally share their books using different levels of independence.

Outcome:
Students will create an ABC book showing different aspects of the Mexico unit that they have found interesting or important. Each letter represents an item they have learned about.

Enduring Understanding:
Aspects of culture affect the development of the social structure.

Essential Question:
What did you learn about Mexican culture?

Type of Lesson:
☑ Literacy Block L1 ___   Mixed Group ___   ESL L2 ✔
☑ ESL L2 (outside literacy block)
☐ Integrated Whole Group

Essential Vocabulary:	Core Vocabulary: Any vocabulary that is appropriate for the entire unit may be used in this project.	Extended Vocabulary:

Activate Prior Knowledge: Teacher will read Mexico from A to Z as a sample book for what the kids can make and share the sample ABC book from a previous unit.	Post-Assessment: Students will share their books with the group as they complete them in an author's chair format.

Materials:
ABC book, white paper without lines, the alphabet printed in very large print for each child, scissors, glue, art supplies for illustration

Description of Lesson:

1. Teacher shows sample of a past ABC book.
2. Teacher and kids brainstorm words they know that start with *A* from the unit on Mexico (e.g., Aztecs).
3. Teacher and students create a chart filled with words from Mexico. As they go, the teacher makes small drawings to make the text accessible to all levels of English speakers. This process can be done at the teacher's discretion, either all at once or over time as the kids work on the book.
4. Teacher models cutting out the letter, gluing it on a blank white page, and making the drawing. Teacher models writing, providing different samples for text such as "*A is for Aztecs.*" Or perhaps more complicated such as "*A is for Aztecs. I learned that the Aztec people built chinamapas to farm.*"
5. Teacher releases students to work.

Differentiation:

Depending on the level of language acquisition the student can choose to share more in depth or the teacher can assist the child by providing vocabulary and scaffolding the information so that the child can still share, using the same language frame for each child.

Resource List/Bibliography:

Kalman, Bobbie. 1999. *Mexico from A to Z.* Crabtree Publishing.

Instead of lists of vocabulary words or labels of innate objects, we use content-based word walls with images. These thematic word walls are often very useful for new English speakers. Instead of thinking of them as isolated vocabulary words, imagine a mural of exquisite art. Each and every piece is interrelated and creates a mosaic on the classroom wall that is useful and purposeful. Word walls based on the theme of study for a specific unit help children access new and prior schema, which allows them to write about what they know or what they are learning. The new vocabulary is connected to the texts being used in thematic integrated units, but words alone are not enough. ELLs need images. These symbolic representations give young writers important clues about what a word means and allows them to work more independently. When the kids create the word wall and see their own images, they take ownership of it and it becomes more useful. These peripheral stimuli let them learn from the environment all the time.

During our studies on Australia and Alaska, Brad types an extensive list of words that are part of the unit's key vocabulary. We think of the vocabulary in terms of essential, core, and extended for differentiation (Shumm, Vaugh, and Leavell 1994). Essential vocabulary words are words that all the kids should know, or have learned before the lesson, perhaps from another lesson or a familiar text. Core vocabulary words are those the kids will need for the lesson and will be learning during the lesson. Extended vocabulary are words they might add to their wealth of words, in essence, enrichment. For example, on a lesson about the Iditarod the essential vocabulary might be *Alaska* and *dog race.* The core vocabulary might be something like *dogs, dogsled, musher, snow,* and the extended vocabulary might be *huskies, harness, runners, veterinarian.* As teams that write and develop curriculum together we teachers decide what the different vocabulary is and in which category it goes. We base our decisions on relevance and difficulty of meaning. All the kids are exposed to all the vocabulary.

To give the kids ownership of the words on the word walls, we cut out the words and glue them on the bottom of five-by-seven-inch sheets of white construction paper. As the kids roll in from an invigorating gym class, we settle them down with a picture walk through the Australian Outback. We read and point to our objective of adding important words about Australia to our word wall. We talk about what we see and any questions that arise. Then we stop at a picture of a kangaroo. We pull out the card with the word *kangaroo* printed on the bottom and begin to model how to draw the picture. We use the picture as a frame of reference, carefully drawing and coloring the kangaroo and its surrounding environment, filling the card with color. Then we post the word on the word wall titled "We are learning about Australia's geography." As soon as we ask for a volunteer, Brayan's hand shoots up. He's new and still hasn't gotten used to using just his thumb instead of waving his arm frantically in the air. He wants to be an

FIGURE 9.3
Brayan draws Queensland to add to our word wall about Australia.

artist when he grows up. "Queensland, I want Queensland!" he says. So we watch as he looks for a picture he can use as a reference. He finds it and immediately begins to run his pencil across the page. Meticulously and with speed uncharacteristic of a seven-year-old, Brayan creates a masterpiece. He shares it with the class and then asks to leave to color it. (See Figure 9.3.) His enthusiasm inspires the other kids to step up and draw spectacular pictures for their own vocabulary words. Everyone has his or her own magical and incredible style. From realistic to abstract they are all artists. We slowly release the children to work on their drawings, providing them with sample pictures of what they can draw. The results are phenomenal. Later the kids write their own vocabulary words as we generate them from discussions, readings, videos, field trips, and guest speakers. These word walls often lead kids to independent inquiry.

Because the kids create the word wall, they are constantly using it to find new words and include them in their writing. Keeping the content word wall interactive is easy. We find that when vocabulary comes up in discussion and readings, we can just find the word and point to it. Because all the vocabulary has a symbolic representation, comprehension is made easier.

Content Time

Content time can be a great time to work on physical geography, build schema through journals or mind maps, or take field trips. All of these things provide greater exposure to information and ideas for inquiries. For example, we love making giant maps for our social studies units. We begin by specifically saying our objective for the lesson and have it posted with a picture for everyone to see. We then begin activating schema by using the word wall to preview vocabulary, talking about our prior readings or discussing field trips, videos, and guest speakers who have shared with us. We can even do a picture walk to spark that prior knowledge.

As appropriate we discuss what is going to be added to the map. We then model how to draw, cut out, and label different parts of the map. We model taking our time and using what we know about the flora. The kids watch as we draw. We release them to work on one part of the map. After fifteen to twenty minutes we return to the group, share, and post our work. This is repeated as attributes are added to the giant map and can occur over several weeks. We take the map down and spread it out. After we have added whatever piece we were working on, we will put it back up. The map always remains visible and accessible. In the next lesson we will, after modeling, add pop-up trees and mountains, buildings, and fauna. (See color insert 8.)

These lessons can be as short as fifteen minutes, and the kids enjoy seeing their thinking around them. Gradually the giant map gets filled with our new learning. We will add a key and a compass rose. Often we have part of our content word wall surround and frame the map. The kids can't help but look at it and read. The map will stay up and surround us for the entire unit. It also becomes a reference point for the kids when they present inquiry projects from the content unit. During the sharing of their research and explorations they step over to the map to emphasize and clarify their thinking to the group. This project has also been a catalyst for some of our students to do individual maps as part of their inquiry projects. Both Kent and Mayra were so inspired by map making that they separately started projects on different regions of the world and without knowing the other was doing it; both made maps as part of the art. (See Figure 9.4.)

The format of planning the lesson looks something like the one on the following pages.

FIGURE 9.4
Kent creates a map of his home country Vietnam after a trip home over the summer.

Unit: Mexico	Area of Study: Giant Map

Lesson (learning focus): Physical geography	Time Frame: Several different class periods over a week.

Content Objective:
Students will familiarize themselves with the geography and maps of Mexico.

Language Objective:
Students will develop an oral capacity to discuss different features of maps.

Outcome:
Students will be able to identify different regions of Mexico on a map.

Enduring Understanding:
Physical characteristics (e.g., rivers, mountains, forests) and human activity shape geographical regions and vice versa.

Essential Question:
What physical characteristics of Mexico influence people's daily lives?

Type of Lesson:
- [ ] Literacy Block L1 ___   Mixed Group ___   ESL L2 ___
- [ ] ESL L2 (outside literacy block)
- [x] Integrated Whole Group

Essential Vocabulary: map, Mexico	Core Vocabulary: desert, central highlands, mountains, coast, city, ocean, key, rain forest, volcanoes, Mexico City	Extended Vocabulary: Gulf of Mexico, Sea of Cortez, Pacific Ocean

Activate Prior Knowledge: Read-aloud, picture walks with nonfiction texts (e.g., National Geographic), discuss family trips, look at map and globe	Post-Assessment: Students will orally share each piece that they add to the map in whole group. Students will also use the map to develop a schema journal about Mexico.

Materials:
Large sheet of white butcher paper, overhead projector, transparency of the map of Mexico, paints, construction paper, crayons, markers, sticky notes for labeling

Description of Lesson:
(Note: This lesson is for Mexico, but could be used for any map work.)

1. Teacher finds desired map to duplicate. One that identifies features of study clearly is best.
2. Teacher makes overhead copy of map.
3. Map is projected on a large sheet of white paper and outlined.
4. Map is cut out and glued to another sheet of paper or can be painted.
5. Gradually information is added to the map. This can be done in small- and whole-group lessons. As information is added, students create symbols to represent that information and add them to the map key. All lessons that relate to map skills can be incorporated by using the large map. This helps celebrate and promote students' thinking and wondering.
6. As the unit progresses, the map is painted and brought to life with symbols.

Differentiation:
Students can depict information on the map both pictorially and with words. Teacher can scaffold by scribing the children's thoughts about each item they are adding so they can add their labels.

Enhanced Learning Strategies:
- ❏ Preview/review vocabulary.
- ❏ Preview/review objective.
- ❏ Use realia.
- ❏ Think-pair-share.
- ❏ Use guarded vocabulary.
- ❏ Use slowed and articulated speech.
- ❏ Use sentence/language frames.
- ❏ Post objectives.
- ❏ Use visuals.
- ❏ Use graphic organizers.

Resource List/Bibliography:
National Geographic

A PERSONAL REFLECTION

Integrating themes throughout the day helps the kids get really excited about their learning. They are able to construct meaning with greater ease, and they are engaged, even if they don't understand every word we say. In the end, we are all working together and having a lot of fun while also looking critically at what is being introduced in the classroom.

CHAPTER TEN

USING ASSESSMENT TO DIFFERENTIATE INSTRUCTION

Through all my experiences with people struggling to learn, the one thing that strikes me most is the ease with which we misperceive failed performance and the degree to which this misperception both reflects and reinforces social order. Class and culture erect boundaries that hinder our vision—blind us to the logic of error and the ever present stirring of language—and encourage the designation of otherness, difference, deficiency. (Rose 1989)

These words remind us of how easy it is to fall into a point of view that adheres to a deficit model. The idea of deficiencies forces us to reflect deeply on our own practices and the ways in which we assess our children. Facing the reality that there is a lot of rhetoric around "gaps" or "the lack of" abilities and knowledge has helped us formulate our belief that no matter where a child is when he or she arrives in the classroom, it is our job to take him or her as far as possible and tap into that child's wealth of knowledge. This is where differentiation plays a huge role.

Differentiating instruction takes place in every classroom; however, in a classroom where there are ELLs, two kinds of differentiation must take place: for complexity of content and for complexity of language. One easy way to facilitate this is to keep blocks of time open for inquiries. Some students will be using fewer sources, others more, but they are all learning in an authentic way. The students have the desire or the spark of wonder, and the teacher is guiding them by explicit and implicit modeling. Some kids will be working more independently and taking notes, whereas others will be with the teacher, who will be scribing their words. ELLs love to explore topics, and there is no reason they should not do so.

As many mainstream teachers may have noticed, there is a wide range of experiences with ELLs, depending on multiple factors such as prior exposure to the language, what language is spoken at home, and the student's educational history. We need to pay close attention to the different levels of language acquisition and what we can do to properly plan for the different levels we find within our classrooms.

In addition to the battery of required assessments our district makes us administer, we use other tools to help us differentiate and evaluate to better inform our instruction. They include the following:

Evaluation of approximations (and self-assessments) to be able to scaffold instruction

Being aware of the different stages of language acquisition and how they affect a student's comprehensible input and output

Transcribing and analyzing student interaction with language

Inquiry checklists

Portfolio development to follow work

EVALUATING APPROXIMATIONS IN ELLS' SPEAKING AND WRITING

Our ELLs are constantly approximating how to express themselves in their new language. This is a great opportunity for us to see what they are thinking and determine the implications it has for our teaching. By noticing their approximations every day we are able to plan how to guide them to the next stage. We notice the nuances of their language and take action to help give them capital in the dominant language of the culture.

Some Approximations We Look For

Transfer of language structures and usage from native language to
  biliteracy

Rhetorical text structures

Use of written and oral language structures in L2

Ability to express ideas clearly

Use of comprehension strategies to construct meaning in their writing

Spacing

Use of conventions

Spelling

We use a format that allows us to look at the strengths of the kids' writing as they take notes and gather information. This frame has helped us look at their notes, notice their strengths and the approximations they make in their writing, and plan by documenting the next teaching points we will use to address whatever we see. We use this frame for inquiry note taking, but it can be modified for any kind of writing sample. We take a sample from one of the sticky notes and put it in the "writing sample" column. We analyze it, write down the strengths and approximations, and decide what the next step will be. This helps us look at what we have addressed with each individual child over time and has been useful in showing how they change over time. (See Appendix, p. 153.)

BE AWARE OF STAGES OF SECOND-LANGUAGE ACQUISITION

Although it might not seem so obvious, being aware of the different stages of second language acquisition has helped us modify our instruction to meet the needs of our students. By being proactive in examining which stage a student is at, we have been able to more accurately understand why children do what they do in different circumstances. Learning more about how we acquire new languages has helped us see our ELLs from a different perspective. It has clarified a number of questions we once had about how and why they interact with us and use language in specific ways. These stages are predominantly based on oral output, and it is important not to confuse a child's stage of L2 (second or other language) acquisition with his or her literacy experience. For instance, a child in the preproduction phase of English language development may have an immense amount of literacy background in his or her native language that affects how that child interacts with and produces texts. It has helped us to keep all these things at the forefront of our minds while planning and teaching. This is simply one way to look at L2 output to help get more insight into what we observe in each individual. The stages we describe below are general and have been developed and modified over the years. We take this information from expanded work done by Krashen and Terrell (1983) on the Natural Order Hypothesis.

Preproduction

During preproduction ELLs might not produce very much speech in English and could be in their silent period, in which they simply listen and absorb the language. At this stage a child is depending heavily on context and beginning to develop comprehension. With these children we use manipulatives, gestures, and realia (real things) to increase comprehension. It is a time when an enhanced learning environment really benefits ELLs, because they are building their receptive vocabulary, or the language they are beginning to comprehend. Some approaches to assessment include substituting written examinations for oral, or using visual assessments such as placing pictures to show order or sequence of stories, matching games with pictures for vocabulary, pointing to objects, drawing pictures, and labeling them (Escamilla and Grassi 2000).

Early Production

In the initial production phase students begin to repeat and continue to listen intently. An ELL may start to produce words in isolation and mispronounce them. We encourage them to communicate with whatever means they feel comfortable using, whether with short verbal responses, gestures, pointing to things, or drawings. We continue to use realia to help with comprehension. They continue to build a repertoire of receptive vocabulary and begin using it more actively. Approaches to assessment similar to those in preproduction can be used with the addition of more text and more sophisticated oral interactions. For example, they may be asked to answer questions using a scaffolded language frame with words such as *who, what, when, where,* and *why.* We can also use performance assessments that focus on higher-order thinking skills while minimizing linguistic demands (Escamilla and Grassi 2000).

Speech Emergence

An ELL in the speech emergence stage might be able to speak in phrases and is increasingly able to communicate. With these kinds of students, activities such as language experience stories, shared writings, listening to stories, and reading books on tape are effective. They begin retelling stories, making comparisons, and contrasting ideas. Comprehension is increasing, and both the receptive and active vocabulary and standard grammatical structures in English continue to become more complex. Assessments should continue to focus on performance tasks, and can have increased text and . . . short-answer written responses or synthesizing (Escamilla and Grassi 2000).

Intermediate/Advanced

By now the ELLs are becoming more sophisticated in their ability to express their thinking by using more complex language structures and have internalized more and more vocabulary. Assessment is similar to the speech emergence stage but grows in sophistication. We have to keep in mind that most ELLs will still not be using conventional grammar and spelling, but are now better able to verbalize their thinking in their new language.

Again, we keep these characteristics of stages of second-language acquisition in mind when looking at kids' work, because it helps us better understand where they are coming from and how to help them move forward.

Self-Assessment

Self-assessment is an important part of the inquiry process because it lets us know whether or not the kids are internalizing the process and the meaning of what they have been doing. It is also a path to independence. Instead of telling the kids what needs to be fixed, we are moving toward "questions that teach" (Johnston 1997). This means guiding the kids to think about what they want their project to be and look like, and to use the strategies we have been working on. These are some of the questions we keep in mind when talking with them about their work to inform both us and them about their thinking:

Talk to me about what you are doing.
How are you organizing your notes?
What do you want others to learn about your topic?
Why did you use these nonfiction features (e.g., labels)?
How did you come up with this design?

This list can go on and on and in fact is constantly evolving and changing. The point is to ask questions or initiate discussions that allow both the teacher and the student to reflect on the work.

HOW TRANSCRIPTS CAN INFORM INSTRUCTION

Although transcriptions are a luxury and can be very difficult to actually do, they can be important in understanding how we and our students use and interact with language. Transcripts provide an opportunity to do in-depth analyses on individual students, on ourselves, on interactions between teachers and students, and on those between the kids themselves. It's sometimes tough to watch yourself, but as Short says, "Looking at ourselves is not particularly comfortable and can be painful. This discomfort is offset by the realization that through careful observation of our talk we are likely to uncover the hidden roles we play and we can become more reflective as teachers" (Short et al. 1999).

Individuals

In cooperation with our teammate Lynne, a transcription of one of our ELLs opened our eyes to what transcriptions can do to help guide our instruction. Alina gave us the opportunity to analyze a myriad of aspects of her language development purely by sitting down with a wordless picture book. By listening to her tell a story we were able to analyze her output in English, the language and grammar structures she was using, her vocabulary and how she used it, her discourse patterns, and how we interacted with her. (See Figure 10.1.) The process of actually transcribing the sessions is very powerful because it allows you to document every nuance, to listen to the student over and over again, and to reflect on what you are hearing.

The implications of doing transcriptions are that as a teacher your awareness of what each child is doing is heightened, therefore allowing you to modify your instruction based on what you see and hear. With Alina, we noticed how sophisticated her L2 structures were, which helped us build on those strengths. Often the approximations made by ELLs are so subtle we don't catch them. By working with Alina we saw that she was inconsistent with the use of the morpheme *s* as a plural and past tense marker, which we hadn't noticed before. This allowed us to specifically address this with her.

We have also experimented with placing a camera on the whole group (including ourselves) to examine how language is being used in conversations among the kids and between us and them. This allows us to see how we interact with the kids (Are we using our discourse routines? What kind of language are we using? Are we using gestures, using images, articulating our speech?), which kids are talking more, how they construct what they want to say, and whether or not they interact more with their peers than

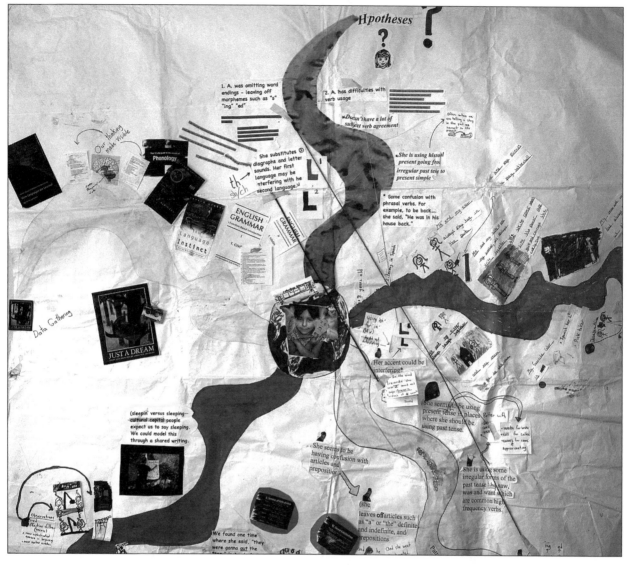

FIGURE 10.1
Alina is the center of a mind map
about her interlanguage or L2.

with us (which shows us that their oral output is developing, just not with us). Another way to analyze language use in the classroom is to film a session of conferring to see what kinds of questions are being asked, how the kids interact with text, to notice if there is a difference in the way they interact with us on an individual level versus in a group setting, and whether the language they use is different. Finally, we sometimes put the camera on just one child who is working on an inquiry to see what happens between the kids during this time of independent work. We often see that kids who are hesitant to share their thinking with us have no trouble talking and sharing with their peers. All of these things give us a greater level of insight than we can get on our own.

PORTFOLIOS

Documenting student work has been important, and we have recently started to develop digital portfolios for our kids. It is important that they see all the hard work they do throughout the year. When thinking about assessment, we have a hard time understanding how scores and grades and getting to the right level on a district benchmark will occupy a space in the hearts and minds of our children. What we do see is that the amazing work they do can be documented and saved for them to share, learn from, and enjoy for a long, long time. "An architect, a designer, an engineer, a teacher, an artist are all likely to have portfolios to show who they are for particular purposes. Very few professionals present test scores as primary indicators of their credentials" (Johnston 1997).

We take a lot of pictures of thinking in progress to emphasize that all this inquiry, writing, reading, and thinking takes time. The digital images allow us to show the process of the kids' work. With blank CDs we are working to make a portfolio for each student to send home and to send on with them to future grades. Printed images are also sent with the CD to accommodate those without computers. Our school has a camera for everyone to share, but we've found we each need one at our fingertips. Pieces for the portfolio can be chosen by the students. As they pick the work they want to save, we sit with them and talk about why it is important, why they chose what they did, and how they went about creating that particular piece of writing or art. We then add these notes to the image so that their thinking is documented. It is a great way to show the change over time not only in their writing, but also in their thinking and how they express themselves.

FIGURE 10.2
We build an anchor chart for the kids to refer to while checking what to add to their posters. Anchor charts enable the kids to be more strategic in their thinking.

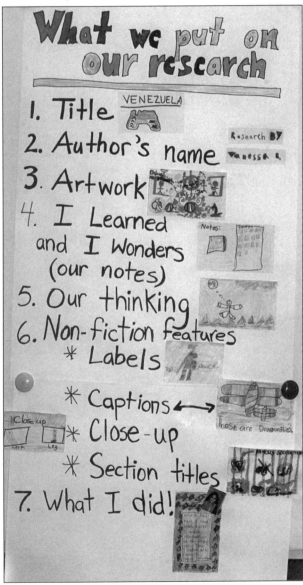

INQUIRY CHECKLISTS

When working with students to evaluate their inquiries we like to keep in mind the characteristics of an inquiry project. Throughout the year we develop an anchor chart that includes the characteristics. Using different-colored paper we write the characteristic, such as "Title," and draw an image to accompany it. We include the date next to it so that we can see when we introduced the idea (Allington and Cunningham 1994). As the year goes on, we slowly add new characteristics, and when we are conferring with students, we refer to the anchor chart so they can check to see whether or not they have included everything. (See Figure 10.2.) The list includes the following:

> Title
> Researched by
> Dedication
> "What I Did." (This is done through a conversation between teacher and student and can be typed to include on the published work.)
> Images to support my text or art to support my thinking
> I used nonfiction features
> I used resources to edit and/or revise my notes and writing.

A PERSONAL REFLECTION

Acknowledging political inequities and racial bias in our world has helped us to speak out against them. To be able to teach and do the necessary assessments we have had to take a step back and examine what we thought we knew about these inequities. Suggestions made by Sonia Nieto in her 2000 book *Affirming Diversity* have been helpful.

To be aware and try to implement new kinds of authentic assessments for ELLs takes a lot of time and dedication, but the manner in which it has affected our lives as professionals and the education of our students has helped us be able to more accurately assess and teach.

We have learned that inquiry is a valid literacy pathway for ELLs and all learners. We believe that it promotes democracy through questioning and engagement by allowing students to follow their curiosities. Teaching through the use of inquiry is a process that is constantly growing and changing. Even as we were writing this book many of the approaches we used in our teaching changed and grew—they got better! Each and every day we learn along with our students. We learn about the topics they study. We also learn what the next steps will be in our teaching. This is part of why teaching has become such a challenging and exciting journey. We have been encouraged to continue to reflect on our teaching and to search for new and better ways to make reading, writing, and learning for our ELLs a meaningful experience that they will continue to explore and build on throughout their lives.

Nieto Suggests

Be familiar with first- and second-language acquisition;

Have the ability to adapt curriculum for students whose first language is other than English;

Be aware of the sociocultural and sociopolitical context of education for students;

Have an awareness of the history of immigration in the United States, with particular attention paid to language policies and practices

Have knowledge of the history and experiences of specific groups of people one is teaching;

Be competent in pedagogical approaches suitable for culturally and linguistically heterogeneous classrooms.

People often ask us when they should start this kind of teaching. Our response is, "Start now!" Start with one student or a small group, and you will find that their energy to explore their world is spectacular!

APPENDIX

USEFUL FORMS

LESSON PLAN

Unit:	Area of Study:
Lesson (learning focus):	Time Frame:

Content Objective:

Language Objective:

Outcome:

Enduring Understanding:

Essential Question:

Type of Lesson:
- ❏ Literacy Block L1 ___   Mixed Group ___   ESL L2 ___
- ❏ ESL L2 (outside literacy block)
- ❏ Integrated Whole Group

Essential Vocabulary:	Core Vocabulary:	Extended Vocabulary:

Activate Prior Knowledge:	Post-Assessment:

Materials:

LESSON PLAN *(continued)*

Description of Lesson:

Differentiation:

Enhanced Learning Strategies:
- ❏ Preview/review vocabulary.
- ❏ Preview/review objective.
- ❏ Use realia.
- ❏ Think-pair-share.
- ❏ Use guarded vocabulary.
- ❏ Use slowed and articulated speech.
- ❏ Use sentence/language frames.
- ❏ Post objectives.
- ❏ Use visuals.
- ❏ Use graphic organizers.

Resource List/Bibliography:

SCHEMA CHART

Name: Date:

My schema about _____ is growing and changing. I learned . . .

QUICK EVALUATION OF WRITING APPROXIMATIONS FOR INQUIRY

Date:

Student's Name:

Strengths	Approximations	Next Teaching Point

IDEAS FOR FORMATTING NOTE-TAKING SHEETS

Date:

Name:

Topic:

Emergent Researcher

I Wonder _____
(I wonder _____?)

My New Schema _____
(I learned _____.)

We like to put images next to the text to help ELLs remember what each column says. We use clip art or our own drawings to enhance the text.

IDEAS FOR FORMATTING NOTE-TAKING SHEETS

Date:

Intermediate Researcher

Name: Topic:

My New Schema
(I learned _____.)

I Wonder
(I wonder _____?)

Wow!

My Connections

Interesting New Words I Am Learning

IDEAS FOR FORMATTING NOTE-TAKING SHEETS

Date:

Name:

Advanced Researcher

Topic:

I Wonder	I Know	My New Schema	Wow!

My Connections	Interesting New Words I Am Learning

Take Action! What I want to do to take action!

Any of these pieces can be added to the Emergent and Intermediate forms based on teacher/student discretion.

PICTURE DICTIONARY

_____
(Topic)

The small box is for the label or caption. The large box above it is for drawing the corresponding image.

COMPREHENSION STRATEGIES

What Are They?

1. **Questioning**

   Readers ask questions to clarify something they don't understand, to resolve problems, to discover new information, and to understand what they read.

2. **Make Connections**

   Readers make connections to their lives, with other texts, and to the world. When children are able to make connections, it helps them understand what they read.

3. **Sensory Images**

   Readers use their five senses and prior knowledge to make meaning from a text.

4. **Infer**

   Readers use their schema and information or clues from the text, to derive conclusions about the text. What do you think will happen?

5. **Determine Importance**

   Readers decide which ideas are the most important in the text. This helps the children determine what parts of the text are of significance and which parts are not as they read.

6. **Synthesize**

   Readers are able to summarize a text, understand its primary ideas, generalize, and develop a new idea, perspective, or way of thinking.

A PARENT'S GUIDE TO RESEARCH AND INVESTIGATION IN THE PRIMARY GRADES

I Learned   I Wonder?

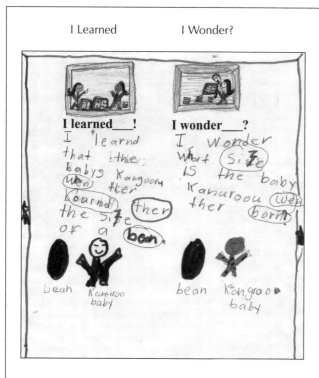

I learned___!
I learnd that the babys Kangoorn (wen) ther (ourmd) the size of a (bean)

bean   Kanuroo baby

I wonder___?
I wonder what (size) is the baby Kanuroou (wen) ther (born)

bean   Kangroo baby

Why Do We Research?

We value kids' thinking and want to give them tools to explore their world.

We encourage kids to be curious—to think and wonder about their experiences, in and out of school.

We encourage kids to read, write, talk, and think about what they are learning, building a classroom community of learners.

Kids are teachers, too. They love to demonstrate and share their thinking with classmates, teachers, and parents!

How Do We Research?

Explore

We build on kids' experiences, whether it's a trip to the desert or finding a weird bug on the playground. Kids get excited about topics they choose. We help them explore curriculum topics through large pictures and photographs, books, videos, real people and real objects, and stories.

Ask

The more we learn, the more we wonder! As we explore the real world, books, and materials, we notice we are learning new things. We encourage kids to use the language of research and investigation to ask questions and record their thinking and learning.

I wonder hurric-anes
how hurrican st starts?

I wonder how hurricanes start?

(Zeke)

Investigate

Kids ask lots of questions as they read books, explore pictures and photographs, explore realia, and transact with text. Once they have questions they want to answer, we support them to find resources that will

A PARENT'S GUIDE TO RESEARCH AND INVESTIGATION IN THE PRIMARY GRADES *(continued)*

help them answer their questions. Sometimes these questions and answers lead the kids to further research. We help them READ and MAKE THEIR THINKING VISIBLE, putting information into their own words and recording their new learning.

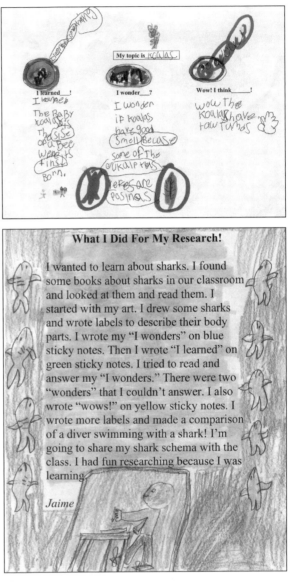

What I Did For My Research!

I wanted to learn about sharks. I found some books about sharks in our classroom and looked at them and read them. I started with my art. I drew some sharks and wrote labels to describe their body parts. I wrote my "I wonders" on blue sticky notes. Then I wrote "I learned" on green sticky notes. I tried to read and answer my "I wonders." There were two "wonders" that I couldn't answer. I also wrote "wows!" on yellow sticky notes. I wrote more labels and made a comparison of a diver swimming with a shark! I'm going to share my shark schema with the class. I had fun researching because I was learning.

Jaime

They use nonfiction features to find information they are seeking in texts.

They read and reread information to see if it answers their question.

They come up with new and often more complex questions . . . and are continually amazed by the new and surprising information they encounter!

Share

Kids share their information to bring it to life. They create posters, write their own books, make a mobile—the sky's the limit! They then share it with all of us.

Act

We encourage kids to take their new learning and act upon it. If we are studying the effects of pollution on Earth's oceans, we can pick up trash around our school to keep our nearby streams cleaner. We can raise money for hurricane victims while studying the effects of weather on people, or even write letters to government officials when we are worried about whales dying because of naval sonar.

PLANES

Unidad: Area de estudio:

Lección (enfoque de aprendizaje):   Tiempo:

Objetivo del contenido:

Objetivo de lenguaje:

Resultado:

Conocimiento que perdurará:

Pregunta esencial:

Tipo de lección:
- ☐ Bloque de lectoescritura L1 ____   Bloque de lectoescritura de ESL L2 ____
- ☐ ESL
- ☐ Grupo integrado

Vocabulario esencial:	Vocabulario central:	Vocabulario extendido:

Activar conocimiento previo: Evaluación:

Materiales:

PLANES *(continued)*

Descripción de la lección:

Diferenciación:

Estrategias de aprendizaje mejoradas:
- ❏ Vista previa/revisión de vocabulario.
- ❏ Vista previa/revisión de objetivo.
- ❏ Uso de elementos reales.
- ❏ Pensar-emparejar-compartir.
- ❏ Usar vocabulario esencial.
- ❏ Habla lenta y articulada.
- ❏ Uso de oraciones y marcas de lenguaje.
- ❏ Mostrar nuestros objetivos.
- ❏ Uso de medios visuales.
- ❏ Uso de organizadores y gráficas.

Lista de recursos/bibliografía:

GRÁFICA DE CONOCIMIENTO PREVIO

Nombre: _____   Fecha: _____

Mi conocimiento previo acerca de _____ está creciendo y está cambiando. Yo aprendí que . . .

EVALUACIÓN DE LA ESCRITURA SOBRE LAS INVESTIGACIONES

Fecha:

Nombre del Estudiante:

Esfuerzos	Aproximaciones	Próximo Punto de Enseñanza

HOJA PARA APUNTAR IDEAS Y PREGUNTAS

Fecha:

Investigador Emergente

Nombre: Tema:

Mis Preguntas

(¿Me pregunto _____?)

Mi Nuevo Conocimiento

(Yo aprendí que _____.)

Nos gusta poner imagenes al lado del texto para ayudar con comprensión.

HOJA PARA APUNTAR IDEAS Y PREGUNTAS

Fecha:

Nombre:

Investigador Intermedio

Tema:

Mi Nuevo Conocimiento

(Yo aprendí que _____.)

Mis Preguntas

(¿Me pregunto _____?)

¡Que Chévere!

Mis conexiones (Este libro/foto me recuerda _____)

Palabras interesantes que estoy aprendiendo

HOJA PARA APUNTAR IDEAS Y PREGUNTAS

Investigador Avanzado

Fecha:

Nombre:

Tema:

Mis Preguntas	Lo que sé	Mi Nuevo Conocimiento	¡Que Chévere!

Mis conexiones	Palabras interesantes que estoy aprendiendo

Tomar Acción: Lo que quiero hacer para tomar acción.

Se puede añadir cualquier sección para investigadores emergentes y intermedios.

ESTRATÉGIAS DE COMPRENSIÓN

¿Qué Son?

1. **Hacer Preguntas**

   Los lectores hacen preguntas para aclarar algo que no entienden, para resolver problemas, para descubrir información nueva y para entender lo que leen.

2. **Hacer Conexiones**

   Los lectores hacen conexiones a sus vidas, con otros textos y al mundo. Cuando los lectores hacen conexiones esto les ayuda a entender lo que leen.

3. **Visualizar**

   Los lectores usan imágenes y crean dibujos mentales para ayudarles a entender el texto.

4. **Inferir**

   Los lectores usan su conocimiento previo e información o pistas del texto para llegar a conclusiones acerca del texto. "¿Qué piensas que va a pasar?"

5. **Determinar la Importancia**

   Los lectores deciden cuales ideas son los más importantes dentro del texto. Esto ayuda a los niños a determinar que partes del texto son significativas y que partes no lo son, mientras que leen.

6. **Sintetizar**

   Los lectores pueden hacer un resumen del texto, entender sus ideas primarias, generalizar y desarrollar una idea nueva, perspectiva o manera de pensar.

UNA GUÍA PARA LOS PADRES SOBRE INVESTIGACIÓN EN LOS PRIMEROS GRADOS

¡Todo lo que aprendí!   ¿Me pregunto?

¿Por qué investigamos?

Nosotros valoramos los pensamientos de los niños y queremos darles instrumentos para explorar su mundo.

Estimulamos a los niños para que sean curiosos, para que piensen y se pregunten acerca de sus experiencias, dentro y fuera de la escuela.

Motivamos los niños para que lean, escriban, y piensen acerca de lo que están aprendiendo, construyendo una comunidad de aprendizaje en el salón de clase.

Los estudiantes son a la vez profesores. ¡A ellos les encanta demostrar y compartir sus pensamientos, descubrimientos con sus compañeros, profesores y padres!

¿Cómo investigamos?

Explorar

La mejor manera de despertar y desarollar el interes por la investigaciónes construir sobre las propias experiencias de los niños, ya sea de un viaje al desierto, o al encontrar un insecto raro en el patio de juegos. Los niños se emocionan con los temas que escogen, o otras veces les ayudamos a explorar temas del plan de estudios a través de grandes pinturas o fotos, libros, vídeos e historias.

Preguntar

¡Mientras más aprendemos, más nos preguntamos! A medida que exploramos el mundo real, los libros y los materiales, vemos que estamos aprendiendo cosas nuevas. En las aulas estimulamos a los niños a usar el lenguaje de la investigación, para hacer preguntas y expresar sus pensamientos y conocimientos.

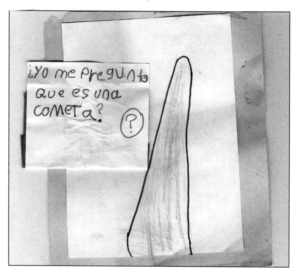

Investigar

Los niños se hacen muchas preguntas a medida que leen libros y exploran pinturas y fotos. Una vez que generan preguntas, quieren respuestas y les guiamos para que encuentren las fuentes que les ayudarán a

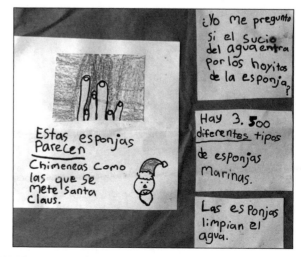

UNA GUÍA PARA LOS PADRES SOBRE INVESTIGACIÓN EN LOS PRIMEROS GRADOS *(continuado)*

responder sus preguntas. Nosotros les ayudamos a LEER y a PENSAR, poniendo la información en sus propias palabras y expresando el nuevo aprendizaje.

Los estudiantes usan características de no ficción para encontrar la información que están buscando.

Los estudiantes leen y releen la información para comprobar si lo que han visto, responde a sus preguntas.

Los niños hacen nuevas preguntas . . . ¡y se sorprenden continuamente con la información nueva y sorprendente que encuentran!

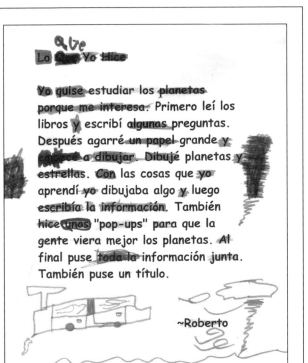

Compartir

¡Los niños comparten su información para darle vida! Ellos crean pósters, escriben sus propios libros, hacen móviles, ¡el cielo es el límite! Luego, comparten con nosotros.

Tomar Acción

Ayudamos a los niños a usar lo que han aprendido y a tomar acción. Si estamos estudiando cómo la contaminación afecta a los océanos, podemos recoger la basura alrededor de nuestra escuela para proteger el medio ambiente. Podemos pedir donaciones para las víctimas de los huracanes durante nuestros estudios de cómo el clima impacta a la gente, o podemos escribir cartas a los oficiales del gobierno cuando nos preocupamos de las ballenas que están muriendo por culpa del sistema del sonar de la naval.

GLOSSARY

Academic Standard: A language variety spoken in schools.

Action: Taking what you learned, or using literacy, and applying it to help transform your world to make it better.

Across Contexts: Changes in learning situations so kids revise and adapt their schema to similar but new conditions.

Additive Bilingual: An environment where bilingualism and biliteracy are valued, encouraged, and taught.

Affective Filter: Krashen's hypothesis of how stress can inhibit the natural process of language acquisition, in turn, thinking and learning.

Anchor Chart: A poster that holds our thinking about a strategy or focus of study.

Anchor Lesson: Initial lessons that launch us into new thinking and schema.

Approximation: When a learner experiments with new schema through reading, writing, or speaking. Students' approximations lead to next teaching points.

Art: Nonprint-based literacy where meaning is made.

Bilingual: The ability to speak/understand (talk of) other languages.

Biliteracy: The ability to read (transact with the text) and write in more than one language.

CLDs: Culturally and Linguistically Diverse students.

Common Language: A learning language and vocabulary teachers and students use to understand each other.

Communicative Competence: The ability to comprehend (input) and express oneself (output).

Comprehensible Input: Krashen's hypothesis about how genuine learning can occur when learning is contextualized and language is accessible.

Comprehension Strategies: Reading strategies that thoughtful readers use to enhance their enjoyment and meaning of the text.

Content Comprehension: The ability to understand overarching themes and ideas in content areas.

Content Word Wall: Vocabulary that is generated through a content unit and is important for our understanding. Words are illustrated with the kids' art to enhance meaning making.

Contextual Learning: Learning that is relevant and meaningful.

Coteaching: Teaching side by side.

Critical Pedagogy: Learning and teaching where schema is learned and revised, and where democracy is promoted.

Culturally Relevant: Teaching and learning which incorporates the students' and families' lives and cultures and promotes democracy throughout the school day.

Deficit View: A stance where students are perceived as lacking abilities, motivation, or schemas.

Discourse Routines: Patterns of talk in the classroom where roles (facilitator, mediator, participant) empower students and democracy is present in our consciousness.

ELL: English Language Learner.

Enduring Understanding: The big and important ideas/themes we want the kids to get from a unit of study. Enduring understandings are used to organize a unit.

Enhanced Teaching: Teaching strategies that aid understanding, e.g., language frames, images, gestures, and so on.

Essential Questions: Questions that surface from important themes of a unit. Essential questions also help frame a unit of study.

Gradual Release of Responsibility: A teaching/learning framework that promotes understanding through teacher demonstration, guided practice, independent practice, and sharing our learning.

Inquiry Based: A literacy pathway that follows kids' natural curiosity.

Interlanguage: The recursive path of learning a new language.

L1: First, primary, or heritage language.

L2: Second or other language.

Language Frame: Explicit language structures that are used to scaffold language development.

Language Variety: A language dialect that has capital where it is spoken.

Literacy Event: Any place or time where literacy happens.

Mind Map: A graphic organizer using art and text to categorize and distribute information around a central theme.

Mini-lesson: A short strategy or content lesson taught through explicit modeling.

Modeling: Teacher demonstrating what the kids will be doing in a lesson.

Narrative: Personal stories based on own experiences.

Newcomer: Recent arrival to the United States.

Outcome: Student-produced work and thinking.

Praxis: How our theory and practice inform one another.

Realia: Real-life objects used to enhance instruction and learning.

Register: Type of talk/writing that varies by setting. For example, talk can be formal or informal.

Research Studio: A place and time for kids to read, write, think, talk, and explore topics of interest. A place where students' thinking is made public so others can respond to it.

Scaffold: A bridge to understanding. Pulling the learner along to more abstract learning through explicit teaching and meaningful activities.

Sharing: A time for kids to share their thinking as a community.

Standard Language: A variety of language that has power in society.

Strategic Reading: Thoughtful readers' repertoire of strategies used to make meaning and understanding through transaction with the text.

Study Print: Cut-apart books or magazines used for instruction, reading, and inquiries.

Team Teaching: Groups of teachers who plan together.

Think-Pair-Share: A discourse scaffold between students where stress is lowered to allow for more talk.

Thinking Disposition: The inclination and sensitivity to know when and how to use your abilities.

Thinking Routine: A routine identified by Ron Ritchhart, that serves to reach broader goals in learning. Thinking routines consist of a few steps, are easily remembered, and are used across academic contexts.

Visible Thinking: Invisible schema made visible through our writing and art.

Writing Studio: A place and time for kids and teachers to write with and for each other. In addition, a place where students' work is displayed and others can respond to it.

REFERENCES

Albers, P. 1997. "Art as Literacy." *Language Arts* 74 (5): 338–350.

Allington, R. L. 2001. *What Really Matters for Struggling Readers: Designing Research Based Programs.* New York: Addison-Wesley.

American Association of School Librarians. 1998. *Information Power, Building Partners for Learning.* Chicago: American Library Association.

Bauer, L., and P. Trudgill. 1998. *Language Myths.* London: Penguin.

Blair, H. A., and K. Sanford. 2004. "Morphing Literacy: Boys Reshaping Their School-Based Literacy Practices." *Language Arts* 81 (6): 452–460.

Bransford, J. D., A. L. Brown, and R. R. Cocking, eds. 2000. *How People Learn.* Washington, DC: National Academy Press.

Bruner, J. 1996. *The Culture of Education.* Cambridge, MA: Harvard University Press.

Buzan, T. 1993. *The Mind Map Book.* New York: Penguin Books.

———. 2005. Buzan™ Unleashing Genius. www.buzanworld.com/the_story_begins.asp.

Cazden, C. 1988. *Classroom Discourse: The Language of Teaching and Learning.* Portsmouth, NH: Heinemann.

Collier, V. P. 1987. "Age and Rate of Acquisition of Second Language for Academic Purposes." *TESOL Quarterly* 21: 617–641.

Cook, S. R. 2005. "Behind Closed Doors: Discovering the Literacies in Our Children's Everyday Lives." *Language Arts* 82 (6).

Crawford, J. 2004. *Educating English Language Learners: Language Diversity in the Classroom.* Los Angeles: Bilingual Education Services.

Cummins, J. 1996. *Negotiating Identities: Education for Empowerment in a Diverse Society.* Ontario, CA: CABE Press.

———. 2005. *Bilingual Children's Mother Tongue: Why Is It Important for Education?* Toronto: University of Toronto. www.iteachilearn.com/Cummins/mother.htm.

Cunningham, P. M., and R. L. Allington. 1994. *Classrooms That Work: They Can All Read and Write.* New York: HarperCollins College.

Dale Easley, S., and K. Mitchell. 2003. *Portfolios Matter: What, Where, When, Why and How to Use Them.* Markham, ON, Canada: Pembroke.

Daniels, H. 2002. *Literature Circles: Voice and Choice in Book Clubs and Reading Groups.* Portland, ME: Stenhouse.

Delpit, L. 1995. *Other People's Children: Cultural Conflict in the Classroom.* New York: The New Press.

Dewey, J. 1916. *Democracy in Education.* New York: Macmillan.

———. 1933. *How We Think: A Restatement of the Relation of Reflective Thinking to the Educative Process.* Boston: D. C. Heath.

———. 1938a. *Art as Experience.* New York: Berkley Publishing Group.

———. 1938b. *Experience and Education.* New York: Simon and Schuster.

Echevarria, J., and A. Graves. 2003. *Sheltered Content Instruction.* Boston: Allyn and Bacon.

Echevarria, J., M. Vogt, and D. Short. 2000. *Making Content Comprehensible for English Language Learners: The SIOP Model.* Needham Heights, MA: Allyn and Bacon.

Education, M. O. 1991. *Dancing with the Pen: The Learner as a Writer.* Wellington, NZ: Learning Media.

Eisner, E. W. 2002. *The Arts and the Creation of Mind.* New Haven, CT: Yale University Press.

Escamilla, K., and C. A. Buxton. 2000. "Toward a Sociocultural Model of Second Language Acquisition." From the Professional Development Resource Series, Second Language Acquisition, BUENO Center, University of Colorado, Boulder.

Escamilla, K., and E. Grassi. 2000. "A Brief Description of Second Language Acquisition." From the Professional Development Resource Series, Second Language Acquisition, BUENO Center, University of Colorado, Boulder.

Ferdman, B. M. 1990. "Literacy and Cultural Identity." *Harvard Educational Review* 60 (2): 347–371.

Finn, P. J. 1999. *Literacy with an Attitude.* Albany, NY: SUNY Press.

Freire, P. 1970a. *Pedagogy of Freedom.* New York: Herder and Herder.

———. 1970b. *Pedagogy of the Oppressed.* New York: The Continuum Publishing Company.

Freire, P., and D. Macedo. 1987. *Literacy: Reading the Word and the World.* Westport, CT: Bergin and Garvey.

Gardner, H. 1983. *Frames of Mind: The Theory of Multiple Intelligences.* New York: Basic Books.

———. 2003. *Art Education and Human Development.* Los Angeles: Getty Publications.

Gentile, L. M. 2003. *The Oracy Instructional Guide: Linking Research and Theory to Assessment and Instruction.* Carlsbad, CA: Dominie Press.

Givon, T. 1993. *English Grammar: A Function-Based Introduction* (Vols. 1–2). Amsterdam: John Benjamins.

Goldberg, N. 1986. *Writing Down the Bones.* Boston: Shambala Publications.

Graves, D. 1984. *A Researcher Learns to Write: Selected Articles and Monographs.* Portsmouth, NH: Hienemann.

Graves, D., and V. Stuart. 1985. *Write from the Start.* New York: NAL Penguin.

Harvey, S. 1998. *Nonfiction Matters.* Portland, ME: Stenhouse.

Harvey, S., and A. Goudvis. 2000. *Strategies That Work: Teaching Comprehension to Enhance Understanding.* Portland, ME: Stenhouse.

———. 2005. *Read, Write, Talk.* Video. Portland, ME: Stenhouse.

———. 2006. *Reading the World.* Video. Portland, ME: Stenhouse.

Heath, S. B. 1983. *Ways with Words: Language, Life, and Work in Communities and Classrooms.* New York: Cambridge University Press.

Hudelson, S. 1994. "Literacy Development of Second Language Children." In F. Genesee, ed., *Educating Second Language Children,* 89–104. New York: Cambridge University Press.

Hurley, S. R., and J. V. Tinajero. 2001. *Literacy Assessment of Second Language Learners.* Boston: Allyn and Bacon.

Johnston, P. H. 1997. *Knowing Literacy: A Constructive Assessment.* Portland, ME: Stenhouse.

———. 2004. *Choice Words.* Portland, ME: Stenhouse.

Jones, S. 2004. "Living Poverty and Literacy Learning: Sanctioning Topics of Students' Lives." *Language Arts* 81 (6): 461–469.

Karolides, N. 1999. "Theory and Practice: An Interview with Louise M. Rosenblatt." *Language Arts* 77 (2).

Keene, E. O., and S. Zimmerman. 1997. *Mosaic of Thought: Teaching Comprehension in a Reader's Workshop.* Portsmouth, NH: Heinemann.

Kohn, A. 2000. *The Case Against Standardized Testing: Raising the Scores, Ruining the Schools.* Portsmouth, NH: Heinemann.

Krashen, S. D. 1983. *The Natural Approach.* Hayward, CA: Hayward Press.

———. 2003. *Explorations in Language Acquisition and Use.* Portsmouth, NH: Heinemann.

———. 2004. "Free Voluntary Reading: New Research, Applications, and Controversies." Paper presented at PAC 5 (Pan-Asian Conference), Vladivostock, Russia.

Ladson-Billings, G. 1997. *The Dreamkeepers: Successful Teachers of African American Children.* San Francisco: Jossey-Bass.

Li-Fang, Z. 2003. "Contributions to Thinking Styles to Critical Thinking Dispositions." *Journal of Psychology* 137 (6): 517.

Lightbown, P. M., and N. Spada. 1999. *How Languages Are Learned.* New York: Oxford University Press.

McLaren, P. 1998. *Life in Schools: An Introduction to Critical Pedagogy in the Foundations of Education.* New York: Longman.

McLaren, P. L. 1988. "Culture or Canon? Critical Pedagogy and the Politics of Literacy." *Harvard Educational Review* 58 (2): 286–309.

Miller, D. 2002. *Reading with Meaning.* Portland, ME: Stenhouse.

Miramontes, O. B., A. Nadeau, and N. L. Commins. 1997. *Restructuring Schools for Linguistic Diversity: Linking Decision Making to Effective Programs.* New York: Teachers College Press.

National Forum on Information Literacy. 2005. www.infolit.org/definitions/index.htm.

Nieto, S. 2000. *Affirming Diversity: The Sociopolitical Context of Multicultural Education.* New York: Addison Wesley Longman.

O'Malley, J. M., and A. U. Chamot. 1990. *Learning Strategies in Second Language Acquisition.* New York: Cambridge University Press.

Pearson, P. D., J. A. Dole, C. G. Duffy, and L. R. Roehler. 1992. "Developing Expertise in Reading Comprehension: What Should Be Taught and How Should It Be Taught?" In *What Research Has to Say to the Teacher of Reading,* 2nd ed., J. Farstup and S. J. Samuels, eds. Newark, DE: International Reading Association.

Pearson, P. D., and M. C. Gallagher. 1983. "The Instruction of Reading Comprehension." *Contemporary Educational Psychology* 8: 317–344.

Peregoy, S. F., and O. F. Boyle. 2001. *Reading, Writing, and Learning in ESL.* New York: Addison Wesley Longman.

Perkins, D. 1992. *Smart Schools: From Training Memories to Educating Minds.* New York: Free Press.

———. 1993. "Teaching for Understanding." *American Educator: The Professional Journal of the American Federation of Teachers* 17 (3): 8.

———. 2003. *The Intelligent Eye.* Los Angeles: Getty Publications.

Perkins, D., S. Tishman, R. Ritchhart, K. Donis, and A. Andrade. 2000. "Intelligence in the Wild: A Dispositional View of Intellectual Traits." *Educational Psychology Review* 12 (3): 269.

Pinker, S. 2000. *The Language Instinct: How Mind Creates Language.* New York: Perennial.

Resnick, D. P., and L. B. Resnick. 1977. "The Nature of Literacy: A Historical Exploration." *Harvard Educational Review* 47 (3): 135–150.

Richard-Amato, P. A. 1996. *Making It Happen: Interaction in the Second Language Classroom, from Theory to Practice.* White Plains, NY: Addison-Wesley.

Ritchhart, R. 2002. *Intellectual Character: What It Is, Why It Matters, and How to Get It.* San Francisco: Jossey-Bass.

———. 2003. "From IQ to IC: A Dispositional View of Intelligence." *Roeper Review* 23 (3): 143.

Rose, M. 1989. *Lives on the Boundry.* New York: Penguin Books.

Samway, K. D., and D. McKeon. 1999. *Myths and Realities: Best Practices for Language Minority Students.* Portsmouth, NH: Heinemann.

Schleppegrell, M. J., M. Achugar, and T. Oteiza. 2004. "The Grammar of History: Enhancing Content-Based Instruction Through a Functional Focus on Language." *TESOL Quarterly* 38 (1): 67–93.

Schumm, J. S., S. Vaughn, and A. G. Leavell. 1994. "Planning Pyramid: A Framework for Planning for Diverse Student Needs During Content Area Instruction." *The Reading Teacher* 47 (8).

Shannon, P. 2004. "The Practice of Democracy and Dewey's Challenge." *Language Arts* 82 (1): 16–25.

Short, K., G. Kaufman, S. Kaser, and M. Crawford. 1999. "'Teacher-Watching': Examining Teacher Talk in Literature Circles." *Language Arts* 76 (5): 377–384.

Singhal, M. 1998. "A Comparison of L1 and L2 Reading: Cultural Differences and Schema." *TESOL Journal* 4 (10).

Strickland, D., et al. 1997. *Language, Literacy and the Child.* New York: Harcourt Brace.

Taberski, S. 2000. *On Solid Ground: Strategies for Teaching Reading K–3.* Portsmouth, NH: Heinemann.

Tishman, S., E. Jay, and D. N. Perkins. 1993. "Teaching Thinking Dispositions: From Transmission to Enculturation." *Theory into Practice* 32: 147–153.

Valdez, G. 1996. *Con Respecto.* New York: Teacher College Press.

Vygotsky, L. S. 1978. *Mind in Society.* Cambridge, MA: Harvard University Press.

Whitmore, K. F., and C. G. Crowell. 1994. *Inventing a Classroom: Life in a Bilingual, Whole Language Learning Community.* Portland, ME: Stenhouse.

Wink, J. 2000. *Critical Pedagogy: Notes from the Real World.* New York: Addison Wesley Longman.

Wink, J., and D. Wink. 2004. *Teaching Passionately: What's Love Got to Do with It?* Boston: Pearson.

Wolf, P. 2001. *Brain Matters: Translating Research into Classroom Practice.* Alexandria, VA: ASCD.

Wolfthal, M. (n.d.). "We Won't Reform Schools by Turning Back: Inequity and Boredom, Violence and Despair Characterized Education in 'The Good Old Days.'" *Educational Leadership* 50–52.

Wood Ray, K., and L. L. Laminack. 2001. *The Writing Workshop: Working Through the Hard Parts (And They're All Hard Parts.)* Urbana, IL: National Council of Teachers of English.

Zinsser, W. 1998. *On Writing Well.* New York: Harper.

On-line Resources

American Association of School Librarians. www.ala.org/aasl.

Bilingual Research Journal. http://brj.asu.edu.

Center for Applied Linguistics. www.cal.org.

Center for Multilingual Multicultural Research. www.usc.edu/dept/education/CMMR/home.html.

Center for Research on Education, Diversity and Excellence (CREDE). www.cal.org/crede.

Critical Pedagogy on the Web. http://mingo.info-science.uiowa.edu/~stevens/critped/index.htm.

Educational Resources Information Center (ERIC). www.eric.ed.gov.

James Crawford's Web site. http://ourworld.compuserve.com/homepages/jwcrawford.

Jim Cummins' Web site. www.iteachilearn.com.

National Forum on Information Literacy. www.infolit.org.

National Council for Teachers of English. www.ncte.org.

National Multicultural Institute. www.nmci.org.

National Clearinghouse for English Language Acquisition. www.ncela.gwu.edu.

Stephen Krashen's Web site. www.sdkrashen.com.

Teachers of English to Speakers of Other Languages. www.tesol.org.

Tony Buzan's Web site (mind maps). www.mind-map.com.

INDEX